AAT

Elements of costing
Level 2
Foundation Certificate
in Accounting
Question Bank

Third edition 2019

ISBN 9781 5097 8119 5

British Library Cataloguing-in-Publication Data
A catalogue record for this book is available from the British Library

Published by

BPP Learning Media Ltd
BPP House, Aldine Place
142-144 Uxbridge Road
London W12 8AA

www.bpp.com/learningmedia

Printed in the United Kingdom

> Your learning materials, published by BPP Learning Media Ltd, are printed on paper obtained from traceable sustainable sources.

BPP
LEARNING MEDIA

Contents

Introduction

This is BPP Learning Media's AAT Question Bank for *Elements of Costing*. It is part of a suite of ground-breaking resources produced by BPP Learning Media for AAT assessments.

This Question Bank has been written in conjunction with the BPP Course Book, and has been carefully designed to enable students to practise all of the learning outcomes and assessment criteria for the units that make up *Elements of Costing*. It is fully up to date as at June 2019 and reflects both the AAT's qualification specification and the practice assessments provided by the AAT.

This Question Bank contains these key features:

- Tasks corresponding to each chapter of the Course Book. Some tasks are designed for learning purposes, others are of assessment standard

- AAT's AQ2016 practice assessment 1 and answers for *Elements of Costing* and further BPP practice assessments

The emphasis in all tasks and assessments is on the practical application of the skills acquired.

VAT

You may find tasks throughout this Question Bank that need you to calculate or be aware of a rate of VAT. This is stated at 20% in these examples and questions.

Approaching the assessment

When you sit the assessment it is very important that you follow the on screen instructions. This means you need to carefully read the instructions, both on the introduction screens and during specific tasks.

When you access the assessment you should be presented with an introductory screen with information similar to that shown below (taken from the introductory screen from the AAT's AQ2016 Practice Assessment for *Elements of Costing*).

> We have provided this **practice assessment** to help you familiarise yourself with our e-assessment environment. It is designed to demonstrate as many of the possible question types you may find in a live assessment. It is not designed to be used on its own to determine whether you are ready for a live assessment.
>
> At the end of this practice assessment you will receive an immediate assessment result.

Assessment information:

You have **1 hour and 30 minutes** to complete this practice assessment.

This assessment contains **10 tasks** and you should attempt to complete **every** task.
Each task is independent. You will not need to refer to your answers to previous tasks.
Read every task carefully to make sure you understand what is required.

Where the date is relevant, it is given in the task data.

Both minus signs and brackets can be used to indicate negative numbers **unless** task instructions state otherwise.

You must use a full stop to indicate a decimal point. For example, write 100.57 NOT 100,57 or 100 57

You may use a comma to indicate a number in the thousands, but you don't have to. For example, 10000 and 10,000 are both acceptable.

The actual instructions will vary depending on the subject you are studying for. It is very important you read the instructions on the introductory screen and apply them in the assessment. You don't want to lose marks when you know the correct answer just because you have not entered it in the right format.

In general, the rules set out in the AAT practice assessments for the subject you are studying for will apply in the real assessment, but you should carefully read the information on this screen again in the real assessment, just to make sure. This screen may also confirm the VAT rate used if applicable.

A full stop is needed to indicate a decimal point. We would recommend using minus signs to indicate negative numbers and leaving out the comma signs to indicate thousands, as this results in a lower number of key strokes and less margin for error when working under time pressure. Having said that, you can use whatever is easiest for you as long as you operate within the rules set out for your particular assessment.

You have to show competence throughout the assessment and you should therefore complete all of the tasks. Don't leave questions unanswered.

In some assessments, written or complex tasks may be human marked. In this case you are given a blank space or table to enter your answer into. You are told in the assessments which tasks these are (note: there may be none if all answers are marked by the computer).

If these involve calculations, it is a good idea to decide in advance how you are going to lay out your answers to such tasks by practising answering them on a word document, and certainly you should try all such tasks in this Question Bank and in the AAT's environment using the sample assessment.

When asked to fill in tables, or gaps, never leave any blank even if you are unsure of the answer. Fill in your best estimate.

Note that for some assessments where there is a lot of scenario information or tables of data provided (eg tax tables), you may need to access these via 'pop-ups'. Instructions will be provided on how you can bring up the necessary data during the assessment.

Finally, take note of any task specific instructions once you are in the assessment. For example you may be asked to enter a date in a certain format or to enter a number to a certain number of decimal places.

Grading

To achieve the qualification and to be awarded a grade, you must pass all the mandatory unit assessments, all optional unit assessments (where applicable) and the synoptic assessment.

The AAT Level 2 Foundation Certificate in Accounting will be awarded a grade. This grade will be based on performance across the qualification. Unit assessments and synoptic assessments are not individually graded. These assessments are given a mark that is used in calculating the overall grade.

How overall grade is determined

You will be awarded an overall qualification grade (Distinction, Merit, and Pass). If you do not achieve the qualification you will not receive a qualification certificate, and the grade will be shown as unclassified.

The marks of each assessment will be converted into a percentage mark and rounded up or down to the nearest whole number. This percentage mark is then weighted according to the weighting of the unit assessment or synoptic assessment within the qualification. The resulting weighted assessment percentages are combined to arrive at a percentage mark for the whole qualification.

Grade definition	Percentage threshold
Distinction	90–100%
Merit	80–89%
Pass	70–79%
Unclassified	0–69% Or failure to pass one or more assessment/s

Re-sits

Some AAT qualifications such as the AAT Foundation Certificate in Accounting have restrictions in place for how many times you are able to re-sit assessments. Please refer to the AAT website for further details.

You should only be entered for an assessment when you are well prepared and you expect to pass the assessment.

AAT qualifications

The material in this book may support the following AAT qualifications:

AAT Foundation Certificate in Accounting Level 2, AAT Foundation Certificate in Accounting at SCQF Level 5 and Certificate: Accounting Technician (Level 3 AATSA).

Supplements

From time to time we may need to publish supplementary materials to one of our titles. This can be for a variety of reasons. From a small change in the AAT unit guidance to new legislation coming into effect between editions.

You should check our supplements page regularly for anything that may affect your learning materials. All supplements are available free of charge on our supplements page on our website at:

www.bpp.com/learning-media/about/students

Improving material and removing errors

There is a constant need to update and enhance our study materials in line with both regulatory changes and new insights into the assessments.

From our team of authors BPP appoints a subject expert to update and improve these materials for each new edition.

Their updated draft is subsequently technically checked by another author and from time to time, non-technically checked by a proof reader.

We are very keen to remove as many numerical errors and narrative typos as we can, but given the volume of detailed information being changed in a short space of time, we know that a few errors will sometimes get through the net.

We apologise in advance for any inconvenience that an error might cause. We continue to look for new ways to improve these study materials and would welcome your suggestions. If you have any comments about this book, please email nisarahmed@bpp.com or write to Nisar Ahmed, AAT Head of Programme, BPP Learning Media Ltd, BPP House, Aldine Place, London W12 8AA.

Question Bank

Chapter 1 Introduction to costing systems

Task 1.1

Look at the definitions below and match them to the correct term, putting a tick in the relevant column of the table below.

Definition	Cash transaction	Credit transaction
Transactions whereby payment is immediate		
Transactions whereby payment is to be made at some future date		

Task 1.2

Look at the definitions below and match them to the correct term, putting a tick in the relevant column of the table below.

Definition	Assets	Liabilities
Amounts that the business owes		
Amounts that the business owns		

Task 1.3

Look at the definitions below and match them to the correct term, putting a tick in the relevant column of the table below.

Definition	Management accounting	Financial accounting
Classifying transactions of the organisation in the ledgers to prepare financial statements		
Analysing transactions of the organisation to provide useful information for management		

Task 1.4

For each of the following activities, indicate whether it comes under planning, decision-making or control. Put a tick in the correct box.

Activity	Planning	Decision-making	Control
Whether to expand the business			
Budgeting how many products to produce			
Regular comparison of actual activities to plans and budgets			
Reporting variances			
Management preparing strategic and operational plans			
Management deciding which suppliers to use			

Task 1.5

Businesses can be set up in a variety of different ways.

Match the description to the types of business by ticking the correct box.

Description	Sole trader	Partnership	Limited company
A group of individuals who trade together to make a profit			
A business where the owner trades in their own name			
The owners delegate the running of the business to directors			

Task 1.6

Businesses make capital or revenue transactions.

Indicate whether the following transactions are capital or revenue by ticking the correct box.

Transaction	Capital	Revenue
Purchase of a motor car for the managing director in a printing business		
Purchase of a motor car by a garage for resale		
Payment of wages		
Rent on a workshop		
Extension works on a workshop		
Office furniture for the managing director		

Task 1.7

Businesses fall into different types based on the different industries in which they operate.

Identify which industry sectors the following businesses come under, by ticking the correct box.

Description	Manufacturing	Retail	Service
Accountants, lawyers and other businesses which don't manufacture or sell a physical product			
The business buys in raw materials for making goods			
The business buys in ready-made goods which it sells on			

Task 1.8

What is the purpose of accounting?

Select the ONE correct answer from the alternatives listed by ticking the box.

Definition	
To make decisions based on the best available data	
To control resources	
To record and accurately classify the transactions of the business	
To find the money to fund the owner's lifestyle	

Task 1.9

The table below lists some of the characteristics of financial accounting and management accounting.

Indicate two characteristics for each type of accounting by putting a tick in the relevant column of the table below.

Characteristic	Financial accounting	Management accounting
It supports managers in their control activities		
In a company it enables the production of financial statements in a format required by law		
It provides information to assist in management decision making		
It ensures that all transactions are correctly classified as relating to assets, liabilities, capital, income or expenses		

Task 1.10

Businesses make capital and revenue transactions.

Indicate whether the following transactions are capital or revenue by ticking the correct box.

Transaction	Capital	Revenue
Installation of new machinery		
Breakdown repairs on a faulty machine		
Fees of bookkeeper		
Purchase of new car for salesperson		

Chapter 2 Cost classification

Task 2.1

Lascaux Ltd makes mosaic tiles for kitchens and bathrooms.

Classify the following costs by element (materials, labour or expenses) by putting a tick in the relevant column of the table below.

Cost	Materials	Labour	Expenses
Glaze for the mosaic tiles			
Gas charges for heating the workshop			
Employees mixing the glazes for the tiles			
Clay used in making the tiles			

Task 2.2

Carcassone Ltd has a bistro and wine shop.

Classify the following costs by nature (direct or indirect) by putting a tick in the relevant column of the table below.

Cost	Direct	Indirect
Wine bought in from a wholesaler		
Business rates for the bistro		
Wages of waiters and waitresses		
Salary of shop manager		

Task 2.3

Lyon Ltd makes guitars.

Classify the following costs by function (production, administration, selling and distribution, or finance) by putting a tick in the relevant column of the table below.

Cost	Production	Administration	Selling and Distribution	Finance
Purchase of strings for making guitars				
Advertising the instruments in the city tourist information shop				
Wages of the bookkeeper				
Salaries of craftsmen making the instruments				
Interest charged on business overdraft				

Task 2.4

Lille Ltd makes bread, cakes and pies for restaurants and its own chain of shops.

Classify the following costs by element (materials, labour or expenses) by putting a tick in the relevant column of the table below.

Cost	Materials	Labour	Expenses
Wages of pastry cooks			
Salesperson's salary for the year			
Confectioner's cream used to fill the pies			
Gas charges for the ovens			

Task 2.5

Look at the costs listed below and indicate whether they are direct or indirect by putting a tick in the correct box.

Description of cost	Direct	Indirect
Factory supervisor's wages		
Lubricant for machinery		
Leather used to make shoes		
Hairdresser's salary in a hair salon		
Telephone rental for administration office		

Task 2.6

Some costs can be incurred for a specific cost centre and some may be incurred for a range of cost centres jointly.

Identify whether each of the following expenses is specific to a single cost centre or is joint, by ticking the relevant box.

Expense	Specific	Joint
Repair of machinery used by one production line only		
Rent of workshop housing three cost centres		
Business rates for the workshop housing three cost centres		
Stationery used by the administration and payroll departments		
Photocopier used by the managing director's personal assistant only		

Task 2.7

Trindle Sewing Machines makes sewing machines. The business has recently received invoices for the following expenses:

Workshop rent	£4,500
Warehouse rent	£2,500
Office building rent	£1,000
Safety testing of the assembly department	£400
Overhaul of the grinding machines	£750
Training for salesperson	£500

The workshop houses five departments, with the following approximate percentage of floor space:

Grinding	30%
Assembly	25%
Testing	15%
Security	10%
Canteen	20%

The warehouse holds the stores and despatch departments, and the stores use approximately 70% of this area.

The office building contains the sales department (one cost centre) and administration, each using equal amounts of space.

Calculate the expenses to be collected for each of the cost centres and insert them in the table below. Show your working in your answer.

Cost centre expense	Working	£
Grinding – rent		
Grinding – overhaul		
Total Grinding		
Assembly – rent		
Assembly – safety testing		
Total Assembly		
Testing – rent		
Despatch – rent		
Stores – rent		
Security – rent		

Cost centre expense	Working	£
Sales – rent		
Sales – training		
Total Sales		
Canteen – rent		
Administration – rent		

Task 2.8

For a manufacturer of hand-made greetings cards, classify the following costs by element (materials, labour or expenses) by putting a tick in the relevant column of the table below.

Cost	Materials	Labour	Expenses
Telephone costs for office staff			
Rent on office building			
Card and paper used by card makers			
Salaries of card makers			

Task 2.9

For a taxi firm, classify the following costs as direct or indirect by putting a tick in the relevant column of the table below.

Cost	Direct	Indirect
Rent of booking office		
Diesel for taxis		
Wages of taxi drivers		
Licence for firm from taxi regulator		

Task 2.10

For a supplier of sandwiches to petrol station forecourts, classify the following costs by function (production, administration, or selling and distribution) by putting a tick in the relevant column of the table below.

Cost	Production	Administration	Selling and Distribution
Wages of workers making sandwiches			
Fee for website maintenance			
Purchases of bread			
Fuel for delivery vehicle			

Task 2.11

Hamburg Ltd processes sausages and other meat products. It has a factory, warehouse and a shop which sells the products.

Look at the costs below and match them to the correct cost centre or profit centre by placing a tick in the relevant box.

Cost	Production cost centre	Service cost centre	Profit centre
Selling and marketing the products in the retail shop			
Mixing, filling and packing the sausages			
Storage in freezers in the warehouse			

Task 2.12

Baden is an accountancy partnership with several offices. Recently the partners decided to set up cost centres to run the partnership better.

Look at the costs below and indicate in which cost centre each would be collected by placing a tick in the relevant box.

Cost	Audit cost centre	Tax cost centre	Personnel cost centre
Payroll software for paying salaries and wages			
Annual purchase of software updated for the year's Finance Act for the tax advisors			
Subscription to an audit advice helpline			

Task 2.13

Look at the statements below and decide whether they are True or False by placing a tick in the correct box.

	True	False
In a service organisation the Human Resources department is likely to be classified as a cost centre		
Distribution would not be a cost centre in a manufacturing organisation		
Stores could be a cost centre in a manufacturing or a service organisation		

Chapter 3 Coding costs

Task 3.1

Alexis runs a successful boat building business within Europe, which exports boats to Asia. His accountant recently recommended a coding system to help Alexis classify his costs and revenues. Each cost or revenue is classified in accordance with the table below. Thus a boat sale to Japan would be 9/200.

Cost	Code 1		Code 2
Sales	9	European sales	100
		Asian sales	200
Production	8	Direct cost	100
		Indirect cost	200
Administration	7	Direct cost	100
		Indirect cost	200
Selling and Distribution	6	Direct cost	100
		Indirect cost	200

Code the following revenue and cost transactions for Alexis, which have been extracted from purchase invoices, sales invoices and payroll, using the table below.

Transaction	Code
Electricity charge for the upstairs offices	
Mobile call charges for sales reps	
Sales to Malaysia	
Sales to Italy	
Brass handles for boat decks	
Factory supervisor wages	

Task 3.2

Mostine Ltd has set up an investment centre for a project it is undertaking over the next few months. It uses an alpha coding system for its investments, revenues and costs and then further classifies numerically as outlined in the first four columns of the table below.

You are required to code the transactions listed in the transaction column of the table below using the code column for your answers. Each transaction should have a five character code.

Activity	Code	Nature of cost	Sub-code	Transaction	Code
Investments	IN	External	100	Bank loan used to set up project	
		Internal	200	Rent on office premises	
Revenues	RE	England	300	Project revenue arising in Edinburgh	
		Scotland	400	Wages paid to project employees	
Costs	CO	Material	500	Proceeds from issue of shares invested in project	
		Labour	600	Materials used in project	
		Overheads	700		

Task 3.3

Alexis has now adopted a new coding system and has been using it for some months now. He has asked you to update the code balances for July using the data below.

Code	Costs incurred in July £
010101	125.00
010102	3,000.40
010103	1,125.80
010202	433.20
010203	1,210.54
010301	44.00
010303	1,450.00

You will need to enter the costs incurred into the table below, which has the opening balances for July, and work out the closing balances at 31 July.

Code	Opening balance £	Update £	Closing balance 31 July £
010101	7,456.98		
010102	6,779.20		
010103	3,556.90		
010201	667.23		
010202	674.55		
010203	5,634.01		
010301	356.35		
010302	362.00		
010303	12,563.98		

Task 3.4

A manufacturer of porcelain and earthenware coffee cups uses a numerical coding structure based on one profit centre and three cost centres as outlined below. Each code has a sub-code so each transaction will be coded as **/**.

Profit/Cost Centre	Code	Sub-classification	Sub-code
Sales	01	Porcelain Sales	01
		Earthenware Sales	02
Production	02	Direct Cost	01
		Indirect Cost	02
Selling and Distribution	03	Direct Cost	01
		Indirect Cost	02
Administration	04	Direct Cost	01
		Indirect Cost	02

The codes have been used for a number of items in November. Identify from each code the profit or cost centre and the sub-classification to which it relates.

Code	Profit/Cost centre	Sub-classification
04/02	▼	▼
02/02	▼	▼
03/02	▼	▼
01/02	▼	▼
02/01	▼	▼
04/02	▼	▼
01/01	▼	▼

Picklist:

Administration
Direct cost
Earthenware sales
Indirect cost
Porcelain sales
Production
Sales
Selling and distribution

Task 3.5

Upp Ltd intends to undertake a new project, the manufacture of school desks, and has set up an investment centre for it. It uses an alpha coding system for its investments, revenues and costs and then classifies them numerically as outlined in the first four columns of the table below.

Code the following transactions for the project, using the table below.

Each transaction should have a six character code.

Activity	Code	Nature of cost	Sub-code	Transaction	Code
Investments	INV	External	214	Sales of desks to Norway.	
		Internal	218	Bank loan raised for project.	
Revenues	REV	UK	428	Telephone costs relating to the project.	
		Overseas	436	Sales of desks to UK schools.	
Costs	COS	Material	870	Wages of desk workers.	
		Labour	945	Wood purchased for the desks.	
		Overheads	975		

Chapter 4 Cost behaviour

Task 4.1

Berlin Ltd makes stationery.

Look at the costs below and classify them into variable, semi-variable, and fixed costs. Place a tick in the correct box.

Cost	Variable	Semi-variable	Fixed
Employee paid a basic wage plus commission based on production quantity			
Rent of the factory workshop			
Print ink used for letterheads and logos			

Task 4.2

Look at the statements below and decide whether they are True or False by placing a tick in the correct box.

Statement	True	False
Many fixed costs are only fixed over a certain range of output		
Variable cost per unit falls as output rises		
Direct costs are generally variable		
Fixed cost per unit rises as output rises		

Task 4.3

Munich Ltd makes outdoor gym equipment. It incurs fixed costs of £50,000 per year in relation to the manufacture of its outdoor treadmills.

Calculate the fixed cost per treadmill at each of the following four output levels and put your answers in the table below.

Output level of treadmills	Fixed cost per treadmill £
1,000	
10,000	
25,000	
100,000	

Task 4.4

Munich Ltd also incurs £35 per treadmill for variable costs in manufacturing the treadmills.

Calculate the total variable cost for the treadmills, completing the table below.

Output level of treadmills	Total variable cost £
1,000	
10,000	
25,000	
100,000	

Task 4.5

The managing director of Munich Ltd wants to know the total production costs for the treadmills.

Use the table below to fill in the figures which you have already calculated and also work out the cost per unit at each level of production.

Units	1,000 £	10,000 £	25,000 £	100,000 £
Costs				
Variable				
Fixed				
Total production cost				
Cost per unit				

Task 4.6

Using the information in row 1 of the table below, complete the remaining rows with the fixed costs, variable costs, total costs and unit cost at the different levels of production.

Units	Fixed costs £	Variable costs £	Total costs £	Unit cost £
1,000	37,200	19,800	57,000	57.00
2,000				
3,000				
4,000				

Task 4.7

A business's single product has the following variable costs per unit.

Materials	£4.50
Labour	£12.60
Fixed overheads	£75,000

Complete the following total cost and unit cost table for a production level of 15,000 units.

Element	Total cost £	Unit cost £
Materials		
Labour		
Overheads		
Total		

Task 4.8

A business makes a single product. At a production level of 27,500 units the business has the following cost details:

Materials	0.2 kilos are used per unit. Materials cost £25 per kilo.
Labour	7,000 hours at £10.50 an hour
Fixed overheads	£35,000

Complete the table below to show the total cost at the production level of 27,500 units.

Element	Cost £
Materials	
Labour	
Overheads	
Total	

Task 4.9

Complete the table below by inserting all costs for the activity levels of 2,000 and 8,000.

	2,000 units	3,500 units	6,000 units	8,000 units
Variable cost (£)				
Fixed cost (£)				
Total cost (£)		24,000	34,000	

Task 4.10

Complete the table below by inserting all costs for the activity levels of 3,500 and 6,000.

	3,500 units	4,000 units	5,000 units	6,000 units
Variable cost (£)				
Fixed cost (£)				
Total cost (£)		34,500	39,500	

Task 4.11

Complete the table below by inserting all costs for the activity levels of 3,000 and 7,500.

	3,000 units	4,000 units	5,500 units	7,500 units
Variable cost (£)				
Fixed cost (£)				
Total cost (£)		31,000	40,000	

Chapter 5 Inventory classification and valuation

Task 5.1

Patties Pastries is a bakery and cake shop.

Classify the following items of inventory as raw materials, part-finished goods or finished goods. Tick the correct box.

Item	Raw materials	Part-finished goods	Finished goods
Fruit cakes left to mature			
Yeast for breads			
Chocolate cakes in the cake shop			

Task 5.2

Patties Pastries wants to calculate the value of its inventory and has been told there are three methods it could use. The table below describes the three methods.

Put a tick against the correct method for each description.

Description	FIFO	LIFO	AVCO
Will give the highest inventory value if costs are rising			
Is the best method if inventories are combined, for instance cake mixes			
Uses the cost of the most recent inventories when costing issues			

Task 5.3

Patties Pastries has issued 100 cake boxes from its stores to the cake shop. Calculate the balance left under the LIFO method using the data below.

Date	Receipts Units	Cost	Issues Units	Cost
April 10	60	£120		
April 11	45	£135		
April 12	25	£75		
April 19			100	
April 27	70	£210		

Complete the table below for the issue and closing inventory values.

Method	Cost of issue on 19 April £	Closing inventory at 30 April £
LIFO		

Task 5.4

Patties Pastries buys in ingredients for its cake mix and issues these to the bakery where the cakes are made. In July it recorded the transactions below. Calculate the balance left under the AVCO method using the data below.

Date	Receipts Tonnes	Cost	Issues Tonnes	Cost
July 5	10	£30		
July 11	15	£45		
July 15	25	£100		
July 19			40	
July 28	30	£150		

Complete the table below for the issue and closing inventory values.

Method	Cost of issue on 19 July £	Closing inventory at 30 July £
AVCO		

Task 5.5

Complete a stores ledger account for the transactions in Task 5.4 using the pro forma below.

	Stores ledger account								
		Receipts			Issues			Balance	
Date	Quantity	Cost per tonne £	Value £	Quantity £	Cost per tonne £	Value £	Quantity £	Value £
Balance at 1 July									
5 July									
11 July									
15 July									
19 July									
28 July									

Task 5.6

A business has the following movements in a certain type of inventory into and out of its stores for the month of May:

Date	Receipts Units	Cost £	Issues Units
5 May	500	1,200	
9 May	1,100	2,750	
13 May			1,450
17 May	400	1,100	
23 May	250	700	

Complete the table below for the issue and closing inventory values.

Method	Cost of Issue on 13 May £	Closing Inventory at 31 May £
FIFO		
LIFO		
AVCO		

Task 5.7

Reorder the following headings and costs into a manufacturing account format on the right side of the table below for the year ended 31 December.

Heading	£	Heading	£
Manufacturing overheads	127,200		
Purchases of raw materials	120,000		
Cost of goods manufactured	570,700		
Closing inventory of raw materials	24,000		
Direct Labour	232,800		
Cost of goods sold	582,700		
Closing inventory of work in progress	24,000		
Direct expenses	102,700		
Manufacturing cost	575,500		
Opening inventory of work in progress	19,200		
Opening inventory of raw materials	16,800		
Opening inventory of finished goods	72,000		
Direct materials used	112,800		
Closing inventory of finished goods	60,000		
Direct cost	448,300		

Task 5.8

Rex Ltd made 150,000 items in a period.

- 375,000 litres of material were used at £0.60 per litre
- 6,500 hours of labour was used at £12 per hour
- Expenses were £105,000

Calculate Rex Ltd's unit product cost by completing the table below:

Element	Unit product cost £
Materials	
Labour	
Direct cost	
Expenses	
Total	

Chapter 6 Labour costs and overheads

Task 6.1

Read the descriptions of labour costs below and match them to the correct term by putting a tick in the correct box.

Description	Basic wage	Overtime	Bonus
Amount paid for ordinary hours of work			
Hours worked above the normal hours stated in the employment contract			
Additional income for working more efficiently			

Task 6.2

Luanne runs a beauty salon and employs three assistants. They normally work a 35-hour week with a basic wage of £8.50 per hour. If they work overtime they are paid this at time-and-a-half.

Use the table below to complete the pay calculations for all three assistants for last week.

Assistant	Hours worked	Basic wage £	Overtime £	Gross wage £
Betty	35			
Hettie	38			
Lettie	41			

Task 6.3

Luanne has now decided to pay her assistants according only to the number of treatments they provide in a week.

The rate used is £15 per treatment successfully completed.

Calculate the gross wage for the week for the assistants in the table below.

Assistant	Treatments successfully completed in a week	Gross wage £
Betty	16	
Hettie	20	
Lettie	23	

Task 6.4

Luanne has decided to pay Lettie a bonus for her hard work.

Using the information in the previous task, calculate how much Lettie would earn if Luanne paid her an extra £1.50 per treatment for the treatments she completed where these exceed 20 in a week. Enter your answer in the table.

Assistant	Treatments done	Gross wage £	Bonus £	Gross wage + bonus £
Lettie	23			

Task 6.5

Luanne has been on a seminar where the speaker referred to the benefits of using piecework and time-rate payments. Luanne unfortunately forgot to take full notes and has asked you to fill in the gaps in her notes, which are in the form of a table.

Refer to the table and tick the correct column.

Payment method	Time-rate	Piecework
Quality is a priority as pay is the same no matter how much is produced		
This method gives employees an incentive to produce more		

Task 6.6

Luanne has adopted a clock card system for her three hairdressers. They are still paid at £8.50 per hour for a 35-hour week. Overtime is now paid at time-and-a-half for time worked in excess of seven hours on each weekday, and double time for any work done on a day at the weekend.

	Hours worked		
	Betty	Lettie	Hettie
Monday	7	8	7.25
Tuesday	7	8	7
Wednesday	8.5	7.5	7
Thursday	7	8	7
Friday	7	7.5	7
Saturday	3	0	2

Calculate the gross wage of the hairdressers based on the clock card information above and enter the details in the table below.

	Betty £	Lettie £	Hettie £
Total hours			
Basic wage			
Pay at time-and-a-half			
Pay at double time			
Total gross wage			

Task 6.7

A business pays a time-rate of £12 per hour to its labour for a standard 40-hour week. Any of the labour force working in excess of 40 hours is paid an overtime rate of time and a third per hour

Calculate the gross wage for the week for the two workers in the table below.

Worker	Hours Worked	Basic wage £	Overtime £	Gross wage £
B Calnan	40 hours			
N Imai	43 hours			

Task 6.8

A business uses a piecework method to pay labour in one of its workshops. The rate used is £2.30 per unit produced.

Calculate the gross wage for the week for the two workers in the table below.

Worker	Units produced in week	Gross wage £
L Akinola	187 units	
J Dunwoody	203 units	

Task 6.9

Jess, Alex and Sid are paid £12.00 an hour and are expected to make 25 units an hour. For any excess production they are paid a bonus of 50p per unit.

Jess works a 35 hour week and produces 920 units.
Alex works 31 hours and makes 770 units.
Sid works 39 hours and makes 975 units.

Complete the table below to show each employee's gross wage for the week.

Worker	Gross wage £	Working
Jess		
Alex		
Sid		

Task 6.10

The following data relates to one year in department A.

Machine hours	25,000
Labour hours	35,000
Units	70,000
Overheads	£350,000

What is the overhead absorption rate per machine hour?

	✓
£5.00	
£10.00	
£14.00	
£25.00	

Task 6.11

Travip Ltd is calculating the unit cost for one of the products it makes. It needs to calculate an overhead absorption rate to apply to each unit. The methods it is considering are:

- Per machine hour
- Per labour hour
- Per unit

Total factory activity is forecast as follows:

Machine hours	20,000
Labour hours	40,000
Units	62,500
Overheads	£500,000

Complete the table below to show the possible overhead absorption rates that Travip Ltd could use. The absorption rates should be calculated to two decimal places.

	Machine hour	Labour hour	Unit
Overheads (£)			
Activity			
Absorption rate (£)			

Task 6.12

The following data relates to making one unit of product H:

Material	3.5 kilos at £4 per kilo
Labour	40 minutes at £18 per hour
Machine time	15 minutes
Overhead absorption rate	£40 per machine hour

Complete the table below (to two decimal places) to calculate the total unit cost.

Cost	£
Material	
Labour	
Direct cost	
Overheads	
Total unit cost	

....

Task 6.13

Perkis Ltd is calculating the unit cost for one of the products it makes. It needs to calculate an overhead absorption rate to apply to each unit. The methods it is considering are:

- Per machine hour
- Per labour hour
- Per unit

Total factory activity is forecast as follows:

Machine hours	40,000
Labour hours	32,000
Units	50,000
Overheads	£400,000

(a) **Complete the table below to show the possible overhead absorption rates that Perkis Ltd could use. The absorption rates should be calculated to two decimal places.**

	Machine hour	Labour hour	Unit
Overheads (£)			
Activity			
Absorption rate (£)			

The following data relates to making one unit of the product:

Material	5 kilos at £6 per kilo
Labour	30 minutes at £24 per hour
Production time	45 minutes

(b)   **Complete the table below (to two decimal places) to calculate the total unit cost, using the three overhead absorption rates you have calculated in (a).**

Cost	Machine hour £	Labour hour £	Unit £
Material			
Labour			
Direct cost			
Overheads			
Total unit cost			

Task 6.14

Rainy Ltd makes two products, the Drizzle and the Chuck. It is trying to decide on an appropriate basis for the absorption of overheads.

	Drizzle	Chuck	Total
Direct labour hours per unit	1.50	2.00	
Machine hours per unit	1.75	2.25	
Total labour hours			80,000
Total machine hours			50,000
Total overheads			£800,000

(a)   **Complete the table below to show the possible overhead absorption rates that Rainy Ltd could use. The absorption rates should be calculated to two decimal places.**

	Machine hour	Labour hour
Overheads (£)		
Activity		
Absorption rate (£)		

(b) **Complete the table below (to two decimal places) to calculate the overhead cost per unit, using the two overhead absorption rates you have calculated in (a).**

	Overhead cost per unit based on machine hours £	Overhead cost per unit based on labour hours £
Drizzle		
Chuck		

Task 6.15

GG Ltd has calculated an overhead absorption rate of £12.75 per unit. Other costs are as follows:

Material	3 kilos at £6 per kilo
Labour	40 minutes at £30 per hour

(a) **Complete the table below (to two decimal places) to calculate the total unit cost.**

Cost	£ per unit
Material	
Labour	
Direct cost	
Overheads	
Total unit cost	

(b) **What would the direct cost be if GG Ltd changed its overhead absorption rate to be based on labour hours?**

	✓
£18.00	
£20.00	
£38.00	
£46.50	

Task 6.16

TM Ltd has calculated three different overhead absorption rates.

Absorption rates:

	Machine hour	Labour hour	Unit
Absorption rate (£)	50.00	33.60	13.00

The following data relates to making one unit of the product:

Material	2 kilos at £4.50 per kilo
Labour	25 minutes at £60 per hour
Production time	15 minutes

Complete the table below (to two decimal places) to calculate the total unit cost, using the three overhead absorption rates.

Cost	Machine hour £	Labour hour £	Unit £
Material			
Labour			
Direct cost			
Overheads			
Total unit cost			

Task 6.17

The following data relates to one year in department B.

Machine hours	25,000
Labour hours	35,000
Units	70,000
Overheads	£350,000

What is the overhead absorption rate per labour hour?

	✓
£5.00	
£10.00	
£14.00	
£25.00	

Task 7.1

Look at the definitions below and match them to the correct term, putting a tick in the relevant column of the table below.

Definition	Budgets	Cost centre	Variances
An area of the organisation for which costs are collected together for management accounting purposes			
Differences that arise when the actual results of the organisation differ from the budgeted results			
Plans of the organisation for the next year in terms of money and/or resources			

Task 7.2

Siegfried Ltd has recently introduced a variance analysis reporting system. The managing director would like you to calculate the variances for the figures in the table, and let him know whether these are favourable or adverse.

Calculate the amount of the variance for each cost type and then determine whether it is adverse or favourable by typing F for favourable and A for adverse in the right-hand column of the table below.

Cost type	Budget £	Actual £	Variance £	Adverse/ Favourable
Materials	24,390	25,430		
Labour	11,270	12,380		
Production overheads	5,340	5,160		
Administration overheads	4,990	4,770		
Selling and Distribution overheads	2,040	2,460		

Task 7.3

It is now one month later and the managing director has asked you to analyse the variances summarised in the table below. You need to indicate whether they are significant or not significant.

In Siegfried Ltd, any variance in excess of 5% of budget is deemed to be significant and should be reported to the relevant manager for review and appropriate action.

Examine the variances in the table below and select the correct option for the right-hand column from the picklist below.

Cost type	Budget £	Variance £	Adverse/ Favourable	Significant/ Not significant
Materials	23,780	360	Adverse	▼
Labour	10,460	660	Favourable	▼
Production overheads	5,330	318	Adverse	▼
Administration overheads	4,220	70	Favourable	▼
Selling and Distribution overheads	1,990	10	Adverse	▼

Picklist:

Significant
Not significant

Task 7.4

The managing director of Siegfried Ltd wants to know more about how budgets work. He has sent you a memo and asked you to confirm whether the statements he has made are correct.

Show if the following statements are True or False by putting a tick in the relevant column of the table below.

Statement	True ✓	False ✓
An adverse variance means actual costs are greater than budgeted costs		
A favourable variance means budgeted costs are greater than actual costs		

Task 7.5

A business has reported actual costs and variances as set out in the table below.

In each case, identify what the budgeted cost would have been.

Cost	Actual cost £	Variance £	Budgeted cost £
Production overheads	12,256	52 F	
Sales and distribution labour	8,407	109 A	
Administration consumables	4,751	236 A	

Task 7.6

A business has identified some significant variances.

In each case, identify the relevant manager that the variance should be reported to.

Significant variance	Manager
Sales	▼
Direct material cost	▼
Expenses	▼

Picklist:

Administration manager
Managing director
Production manager
Sales manager
Training manager

Task 7.7

In each case, identify whether the statement is true or false.

Statement	True/False
A significant variance in the selling and distribution overheads should be reported to the sales manager	▼
A significant variance in the labour cost should be reported to the production manager and the human resources manager	▼
A significant variance in production overheads should be reported to the production manager	▼
A significant variance in the sales income should be reported to the production manager	▼

Picklist:

True
False

Task 7.8

Last month's performance report for Kite Ltd is summarised in the table below. Any variance in excess of 5% of budget is deemed to be significant and should be reported to the relevant managers for review and appropriate action.

(a) **Examine the variances in the table and then determine whether they are significant or not by making a selection in the relevant column below.**

Cost	Budget £	Variance £	
Direct material Department A	10,200	500	▼
Direct material Department B	9,800	600	▼
Direct labour Department A	11,300	400	▼
Direct labour Department B	7,500	400	▼

Picklist:

Significant
Not significant

(b) **Identify whether the following statements are true or false.**

Statement	
The variance for the Direct Material cost of Department A should be reported to the purchasing manager.	▼
The variance for the Direct Labour cost of Department B should be reported to the production manager for Department B.	▼
The variance for the Direct Labour cost of Department A should be reported to the sales manager.	▼
The variance for the Direct Material cost of Department B should be reported to the production manager for Department B.	▼

Picklist:

True
False

Answer Bank

BPP
LEARNING MEDIA

Chapter 1 Introduction to costing systems

Task 1.1

Definition	Cash transaction	Credit transaction
Transactions whereby payment is immediate	✓	
Transactions whereby payment is to be made at some future date		✓

Task 1.2

Definition	Assets	Liabilities
Amounts that the business owes		✓
Amounts that the business owns	✓	

Task 1.3

Definition	Management accounting	Financial accounting
Classifying transactions of the organisation in the ledgers to prepare financial statements		✓
Analysing transactions of the organisation to provide useful information for management	✓	

Task 1.4

Activity	Planning	Decision-making	Control
Whether to expand the business		✓	
Budgeting how many products to produce	✓		
Regular comparison of actual activities to plans and budgets			✓
Reporting variances			✓
Management preparing strategic and operational plans	✓		
Management deciding which suppliers to use		✓	

Task 1.5

Description	Sole trader	Partnership	Limited company
A group of individuals who trade together to make a profit		✓	
A business where the owner trades in their own name	✓		
The owners delegate the running of the business to directors			✓

Task 1.6

Transaction	Capital	Revenue
Purchase of a motor car for the managing director in a printing business	✓	
Purchase of a motor car by a garage for resale		✓
Payment of wages		✓
Rent on a workshop		✓
Extension works on a workshop	✓	
Office furniture for the managing director	✓	

Task 1.7

Description	Manufacturing	Retail	Service
Accountants, lawyers and other businesses which don't manufacture or sell a physical product			✓
The business buys in raw materials for making goods	✓		
The business buys in ready-made goods which it sells on		✓	

Task 1.8

Definition	✓
To make decisions based on the best available data	
To control resources	
To record and accurately classify the transactions of the business	✓
To find the money to fund the owner's lifestyle	

Task 1.9

Characteristic	Financial accounting	Management accounting
It supports managers in their control activities		✓
In a company it enables the production of financial statements in a format required by law	✓	
It provides information to assist in management decision making		✓
It ensures that all transactions are correctly classified as relating to assets, liabilities, capital, income or expenses	✓	

Task 1.10

Transaction	Capital	Revenue
Installation of new machinery	✓	
Breakdown repairs on a faulty machine		✓
Fees of bookkeeper		✓
Purchase of new car for salesperson	✓	

Chapter 2 Cost classification

Task 2.1

Cost	Materials	Labour	Expenses
Glaze for the mosaic tiles	✓		
Gas charges for heating the workshop			✓
Employees mixing the glazes for the tiles		✓	
Clay used in making the tiles	✓		

Task 2.2

Cost	Direct	Indirect
Wine bought in from a wholesaler	✓	
Business rates for the bistro		✓
Wages of waiters and waitresses	✓	
Salary of shop manager		✓

Task 2.3

Cost	Production	Administration	Selling and distribution	Finance
Purchase of strings for making guitars	✓			
Advertising the instruments in the city tourist information shop			✓	
Wages of the bookkeeper		✓		
Salaries of craftsmen making the instruments	✓			
Interest charged on business overdraft				✓

Task 2.4

Cost	Materials	Labour	Expenses
Wages of pastry cooks		✓	
Salesperson's salary for the year		✓	
Confectioner's cream used to fill the pies	✓		
Gas charges for the ovens			✓

Task 2.5

Description of cost	Direct	Indirect
Factory supervisor's wages		✓
Lubricant for machinery		✓
Leather used to make shoes	✓	
Hairdresser's salary in a hair salon	✓	
Telephone rental for administration office		✓

Task 2.6

Expense	Specific	Joint
Repair of machinery used by one production line only	✓	
Rent of workshop housing three cost centres		✓
Business rates for the workshop housing three cost centres		✓
Stationery used by the administration and payroll departments		✓
Photocopier used by the managing director's personal assistant only	✓	

Task 2.7

Cost centre expense	Working	£
Grinding – rent	£4,500 × 30%	1,350
Grinding – overhaul		750
Total Grinding		2,100
Assembly – rent	£4,500 × 25%	1,125
Assembly – safety testing		400
Total Assembly		1,525
Testing – rent	£4,500 × 15%	675
Despatch – rent	£2,500 × 30%	750
Stores – rent	£2,500 × 70%	1,750
Security – rent	£4,500 × 10%	450
Sales – rent	£1,000 × 50%	500
Sales – training		500
Total Sales		1,000
Canteen – rent	£4,500 × 20%	900
Administration – rent	£1,000 × 50%	500

Task 2.8

Cost	Materials	Labour	Expenses
Telephone costs for office staff			✓
Rent on office building			✓
Card and paper used by card makers	✓		
Salaries of card makers		✓	

Task 2.9

Cost	Direct	Indirect
Rent of booking office		✓
Diesel for taxis	✓	
Wages of taxi drivers	✓	
Licence for firm from taxi regulator		✓

Task 2.10

Cost	Production	Administration	Selling and distribution
Wages of workers making sandwiches	✓		
Fee for website maintenance		✓	
Purchases of bread	✓		
Fuel for delivery vehicle			✓

Task 2.11

Cost	Production cost centre	Service cost centre	Profit centre
Selling and marketing the products in the retail shop			✓
Mixing, filling and packing the sausages	✓		
Storage in freezers in the warehouse		✓	

Task 2.12

Cost	Audit cost centre	Tax cost centre	Personnel cost centre
Payroll software for paying salaries and wages			✓
Annual purchase of software updated for the year's Finance Act for the tax advisors		✓	
Subscription to an audit advice helpline	✓		

Task 2.13

	True	False
In a service organisation the Human Resources department is likely to be classified as a cost centre	✓	
Distribution would not be a cost centre in a manufacturing organisation		✓
Stores could be a cost centre in a manufacturing or a service organisation	✓	

Chapter 3 Coding costs

Task 3.1

Transaction	Code
Electricity charge for the upstairs offices	7/200
Mobile call charges for sales reps	6/200
Sales to Malaysia	9/200
Sales to Italy	9/100
Brass handles for boat decks	8/100
Factory supervisor wages	8/200

Task 3.2

Activity	Code	Nature of cost	Sub-code		Transaction	Code
Investments	IN	External	100		Bank loan used to set up project	IN100
		Internal	200		Rent on office premises	CO700
Revenues	RE	England	300		Project revenue arising in Edinburgh	RE400
		Scotland	400		Wages paid to project employees	CO600
Costs	CO	Material	500		Proceeds from issue of shares invested in project	IN200
		Labour	600		Materials used in project	CO500
		Overheads	700			

Task 3.3

Code	Opening balance £	Update £	Closing balance 31 July £
010101	7,456.98	125.00	7,581.98
010102	6,779.20	3,000.40	9,779.60
010103	3,556.90	1,125.80	4,682.70
010201	667.23	0	667.23
010202	674.55	433.20	1,107.75
010203	5,634.01	1,210.54	6,844.55
010301	356.35	44.00	400.35
010302	362.00	0	362.00
010303	12,563.98	1,450.00	14,013.98

Task 3.4

Code	Profit/Cost centre	Sub-classification
04/02	Administration	Indirect cost
02/02	Production	Indirect cost
03/02	Selling and distribution	Indirect cost
01/02	Sales	Earthenware sales
02/01	Production	Direct cost
04/02	Administration	Indirect cost
01/01	Sales	Porcelain sales

Task 3.5

Activity	Code	Nature of cost	Sub-code		Transaction	Code
Investments	INV	External	214		Sales of desks to Norway.	REV436
		Internal	218		Bank loan raised for project.	INV214
Revenues	REV	UK	428		Telephone costs relating to the project.	COS975
		Overseas	436		Sales of desks to UK schools.	REV428
Costs	COS	Material	870		Wages of desk workers.	COS945
		Labour	945		Wood purchased for the desks.	COS870
		Overheads	975			

Chapter 4 Cost behaviour

Task 4.1

Cost	Variable	Semi-variable	Fixed
Employee paid a basic wage plus commission based on production quantity		✓	
Rent of the factory workshop			✓
Print ink used for letterheads and logos	✓		

Task 4.2

Statement	True	False
Many fixed costs are only fixed over a certain range of output	✓	
Variable cost per unit falls as output rises		✓
Direct costs are generally variable	✓	
Fixed cost per unit rises as output rises		✓

Task 4.3

Output level of treadmills	Fixed cost per treadmill £
1,000	50
10,000	5
25,000	2
100,000	0.50

Task 4.4

Output level of treadmills	Total variable cost £
1,000	35,000
10,000	350,000
25,000	875,000
100,000	3,500,000

Task 4.5

Units	1,000 £	10,000 £	25,000 £	100,000 £
Costs				
Variable (units × (£35))	35,000	350,000	875,000	3,500,000
Fixed	50,000	50,000	50,000	50,000
Total production cost	85,000	400,000	925,000	3,550,000
Cost per unit	£85.00	£40.00	£37.00	£35.50

Task 4.6

Units	Fixed costs £	Variable costs £	Total costs £	Unit cost £
1,000	37,200	19,800	57,000	57.00
2,000	37,200	39,600	76,800	38.40
3,000	37,200	59,400	96,600	32.20
4,000	37,200	79,200	116,400	29.10

Task 4.7

Element	Total cost £	Unit cost £
Materials	67,500	4.50
Labour	189,000	12.60
Overheads	75,000	5.00
Total	331,500	22.10

Task 4.8

Element	Cost £
Materials	137,500
Labour	73,500
Overheads	35,000
Total	246,000

Task 4.9

	2,000 units	3,500 units	6,000 units	8,000 units
Variable cost (£)	8,000			32,000
Fixed cost (£)	10,000			10,000
Total cost (£)	18,000	24,000	34,000	42,000

Workings

Variable cost per unit = (£34,000 – £24,000)/(6,000 – 3,500) = £4 per unit
Fixed cost = £34,000 – (6,000 × £4) = £10,000
Variable cost of 2,000 units = (2,000 × £4) = £8,000
Variable cost of 8,000 units = (8,000 × £4) = £32,000

Task 4.10

	3,500 units	4,000 units	5,000 units	6,000 units
Variable cost (£)	17,500			30,000
Fixed cost (£)	14,500			14,500
Total cost (£)	32,000	34,500	39,500	44,500

Workings

Variable cost per unit = (£39,500 – £34,500)/(5,000 – 4,000) = £5 per unit
Fixed cost = £34,500 – (4,000 × £5) = £14,500
Variable cost of 3,500 units = (3,500 × £5) = £17,500
Variable cost of 6,000 units = (6,000 × £5) = £30,000

Task 4.11

	3,000 units	4,000 units	5,500 units	7,500 units
Variable cost (£)	18,000			45,000
Fixed cost (£)	7,000			7,000
Total cost (£)	25,000	31,000	40,000	52,000

Workings

Variable cost per unit = (£40,000 – £31,000)/(5,500 – 4,000) = £6 per unit
Fixed cost = £40,000 – (5,500 × £6) = £7,000
Variable cost of 3,000 units = (3,000 × £6) = £18,000
Variable cost of 7,500 units = (7,500 × £6) = £45,000

Chapter 5 Inventory classification and valuation

Task 5.1

Item	Raw materials	Part-finished goods	Finished goods
Fruit cakes left to mature		✓	
Yeast for breads	✓		
Chocolate cakes in the cake shop			✓

Task 5.2

Description	FIFO	LIFO	AVCO
Will give the highest inventory value if costs are rising	✓		
Is the best method if inventories are combined, for instance cake mixes			✓
Uses the cost of the most recent inventories when costing issues		✓	

Task 5.3

The cost of the issue on 19 April under LIFO is £75 + £135 + (30 × £120/60) = £270.

Closing inventory at 30 April consists of 30 units at £120/60 = £60, plus the receipt of 70 units for £210.

Method	Cost of issue on 19 April £	Closing inventory at 30 April £
LIFO	270	270

Task 5.4

The cost of the issue on 19 July under AVCO is (£30 + £45 + £100)/(10 + 15 + 25) × 40 = £140.

Closing inventory at 30 July consists of 10 units at £175/50 = £35, plus the receipt of 30 units for £150.

Method	Cost of issue on 19 July £	Closing inventory at 30 July £
AVCO	140	185

Task 5.5

Stores ledger account	Receipts			Issues			Balance	
Date	Quantity	Cost per tonne £	Value £	Quantity £	Cost per tonne £	Value £	Quantity £	Value £
Balance at 1 July							0	0
5 July	10	3.00	30				10	30
11 July	15	3.00	45				25	75
15 July	25	4.00	100				50	175
19 July				40	3.50	140	10	35
28 July	30	5.00	150				40	185

Task 5.6

Method	Cost of issue on 13 May £	Closing inventory at 31 May £
FIFO	1,200 + (950 × 2,750/1,100) = **3,575**	700 + 1,100 + (150 × 2,750/1,100) = **2,175**
LIFO	2,750 + (350 × 1,200/500) = **3,590**	700 + 1,100 + (150 × 1,200/500) = **2,160**
AVCO	1,450/1,600 × (1,200 + 2,750) = **3,580**	700 + 1,100 + (150/1,600 × (1,200 + 2,750)) = **2,170**

Task 5.7

Heading	£	Heading	£
Manufacturing overheads	127,200	Opening Inventory of Raw Materials	16,800
Purchases of raw materials	120,000	Purchases of Raw Materials	120,000
Cost of goods manufactured	570,700	Closing Inventory of Raw Materials	24,000
Closing inventory of raw materials	24,000	Direct materials used	112,800
Direct Labour	232,800	Direct Labour	232,800
Cost of goods sold	582,700	Direct Expenses	102,700
Closing inventory of work in progress	24,000	Direct cost	448,300
Direct expenses	102,700	Manufacturing Overheads	127,200

Heading	£	Heading	£
Manufacturing cost	575,500	Manufacturing cost	575,500
Opening inventory of work in progress	19,200	Opening Inventory of Work in Progress	19,200
Opening inventory of raw materials	16,800	Closing Inventory of Work in Progress	24,000
Opening inventory of finished goods	72,000	Cost of goods manufactured	570,700
Direct materials used	112,800	Opening Inventory of Finished Goods	72,000
Closing inventory of finished goods	60,000	Closing Inventory of Finished Goods	60,000
Direct cost	448,300	Cost of goods sold	582,700

Task 5.8

Element	Workings	Unit product cost £
Materials	(375,000 × £0.60)/150,000	1.50
Labour	(6,500 × £12)/150,000	0.52
Direct cost		2.02
Expenses	£105,000/150,000	0.70
Total		2.72

Chapter 6 Labour costs and overheads

Task 6.1

Description	Basic wage	Overtime	Bonus
Amount paid for ordinary hours of work	✓		
Hours worked above the normal hours stated in the employment contract		✓	
Additional income for working more efficiently			✓

Task 6.2

Assistant	Hours worked	Basic wage £	Overtime £	Gross wage £
Betty	35	297.50	0	297.50
Hettie	38	297.50	38.25	335.75
Lettie	41	297.50	76.50	374.00

Task 6.3

Assistant	Treatments successfully completed in a week	Gross wage £
Betty	16	240
Hettie	20	300
Lettie	23	345

Task 6.4

Assistant	Treatments done	Gross wage £	Bonus £	Gross wage + bonus £
Lettie	23	345	4.50	349.50

Task 6.5

Payment method	Time-rate	Piecework
Quality is a priority as pay is the same no matter how much is produced	✓	
This method gives employees an incentive to produce more		✓

Task 6.6

	Betty £	Lettie £	Hettie £
Total hours	**39.50**	**39.00**	**37.25**
Basic wage (35 × £8.50)	**297.50**	**297.50**	**297.50**
Pay at time-and-a-half	1.5 × 8.50 × 1.5 = **19.12**	4 × 8.50 × 1.5 = **51.00**	0.25 × 8.50 × 1.5 = **3.19**
Pay at double time	3 × 8.50 × 2 = **51.00**	0	2 × 8.50 × 2 = **34.00**
Total gross wage	**367.62**	**348.50**	**334.69**

Task 6.7

Worker	Hours worked	Basic wage £	Overtime £	Gross wage £
B Calnan	40 hours	480.00	0	480.00
N Imai	43 hours	480.00	48.00	528.00

Task 6.8

Worker	Units produced in week	Gross wage £
L Akinola	187 units	430.10
J Dunwoody	203 units	466.90

Task 6.9

Worker	Gross wage £	Working
Jess	442.50	Expected: 35 × 25 = 875 units. Receives bonus for (920 – 875) = 45 units at 50p per unit. So gross wage is (35 × £12) + (45 × £0.5) = 442.50
Alex	372.00	Expected: 31 × 25 = 775 units. Receives no bonus as made fewer than expected. So gross wage is 31 × £12 = £372
Sid	468.00	Expected: 39 × 25 = 975 units. Receives no bonus as made quantity expected. So gross wage is 39 × £12 = £468

Task 6.10

£350,000/25,000 = £14.00

Task 6.11

	Machine hour	Labour hour	Unit
Overheads (£)	500,000	500,000	500,000
Activity	20,000	40,000	62,500
Absorption rate (£)	25.00	12.50	8.00

Task 6.12

Cost	£
Material	14.00
Labour	12.00
Direct cost	26.00
Overheads	10.00
Total unit cost	36.00

Workings

Material = 3.5 kilos × £4 = £14.00
Labour = (40/60) hours × £18 = £12.00
Direct cost = material + labour = £14.00 + £12.00 = £26.00
Overheads = (15/60) hours × £40 = £10.00

Task 6.13

(a)

	Machine hour	Labour hour	Unit
Overheads (£)	400,000	400,000	400,000
Activity	40,000	32,000	50,000
Absorption rate (£)	10.00	12.50	8.00

(b)

Cost	Machine hour £	Labour hour £	Unit £
Material	30.00	30.00	30.00
Labour	12.00	12.00	12.00
Direct cost	42.00	42.00	42.00
Overheads	7.50	6.25	8.00
Total unit cost	49.50	48.25	50.00

Workings

Material = 5 kilos × £6 = £30.00
Labour = (30/60) hours × £24 = £12.00
Direct cost = material + labour = £30.00 + £12.00 = £42.00
Overheads based on machine hours = (45/60) hours × £10 = £7.50
Overheads based on labour hours = (30/60) hours × £12.50 = £6.25
Overheads based on number of units = 1 × £8.00 = £8.00

Task 6.14

(a)

	Machine hour	Labour hour
Overheads (£)	800,000	800,000
Activity	50,000	80,000
Absorption rate (£)	16.00	10.00

(b)

	Overhead cost per unit based on machine hours £	Overhead cost per unit based on labour hours £
Drizzle	28.00	15.00
Chuck	36.00	20.00

Workings

Overheads based on machine hours
Drizzle = 1.75 hours × £16.00 = £28.00
Chuck = 2.25 hours × £16.00 = £36.00
Overheads based on labour hours
Drizzle = 1.50 hours × £10.00 = £15.00
Chuck = 2.00 hours × £10.00 = £20.00

Task 6.15

(a)

Cost	£ per unit
Material	18.00
Labour	20.00
Direct cost	38.00
Overheads	12.75
Total unit cost	50.75

(b) £38.00 The direct cost would remain the same (material + labour = £18.00 + £20.00 = £38.00)

Task 6.16

Cost	Machine hour £	Labour hour £	Unit £
Material	9.00	9.00	9.00
Labour	25.00	25.00	25.00
Direct cost	34.00	34.00	34.00
Overheads	12.50	14.00	13.00
Total unit cost	46.50	48.00	47.00

Workings

Material = 2 kgs × £4.50 = £9.00
Labour = (25/60) hours × £60 = £25.00
Direct cost = material + labour = £9.00 + £25.00 = £34.00
Overheads based on machine hours = (15/60) hours × £50 = £12.50
Overheads based on labour hours = (25/60) hours × £33.60 = £14.00
Overheads based on number of units = 1 × £13.00 = £13.00

Task 6.17

£350,000/35,000 = £10.00

Task 7.1

Definition	Budgets	Cost centre	Variances
An area of the organisation for which costs are collected together for management accounting purposes		✓	
Differences that arise when the actual results of the organisation differ from the budgeted results			✓
Plans of the organisation for the next year in terms of money and/or resources	✓		

Task 7.2

Cost type	Budget £	Actual £	Variance £	Adverse/ Favourable
Materials	24,390	25,430	1,040	A
Labour	11,270	12,380	1,110	A
Production overheads	5,340	5,160	180	F
Administration overheads	4,990	4,770	220	F
Selling and Distribution overheads	2,040	2,460	420	A

Task 7.3

Cost type	Budget £	Variance £	Adverse/ Favourable	Significant/ Not significant
Materials	23,780	360	Adverse	Not significant
Labour	10,460	660	Favourable	Significant
Production overheads	5,330	318	Adverse	Significant
Administration overheads	4,220	70	Favourable	Not significant
Selling and Distribution overheads	1,990	10	Adverse	Not significant

Task 7.4

Statement	True	False
An adverse variance means actual costs are greater than budgeted costs	✓	
A favourable variance means budgeted costs are greater than actual costs	✓	

Task 7.5

Cost	Actual cost £	Variance £	Budgeted cost £
Production overheads	12,256	52 F	12,308
Sales and distribution labour	8,407	109 A	8,298
Administration consumables	4,751	236 A	4,515

Task 7.6

Significant variance	Manager
Sales	Sales manager
Direct material cost	Production manager
Expenses	Administration manager

Task 7.7

Statement	True/False
A significant variance in the selling and distribution overheads should be reported to the sales manager	True
A significant variance in the labour cost should be reported to the production manager and the human resources manager	True
A significant variance in production overheads should be reported to the production manager	True
A significant variance in the sales income should be reported to the production manager	False

A significant variance in the sales income should be reported to the sales manager.

Task 7.8

(a)

Cost	Budget £	Variance £	
Direct material Department A	10,200	500	Not significant
Direct material Department B	9,800	600	Significant
Direct labour Department A	11,300	400	Not significant
Direct labour Department B	7,500	400	Significant

Workings

500/10,200 × 100% = 4.9% – not significant
600/9,800 × 100% = 6.1% – significant
400/11,300 × 100% = 3.5% – not significant
400/7,500 × 100% = 5.3% – significant

(b)

Statement	
The variance for the Direct Material cost of Department A should be reported to the purchasing manager.	False
The variance for the Direct Labour cost of Department B should be reported to the production manager for Department B.	True
The variance for the Direct Labour cost of Department A should be reported to the sales manager.	False
The variance for the Direct Material cost of Department B should be reported to the production manager for Department A.	False

The variance for direct material Department A is not significant and so should not be reported.

The variance for direct labour Department B is significant. It should be reported to the production manager for Department B.

The variance for the direct labour Department A is not significant and so should not be reported.

The variance for direct material Department B is significant but it should be reported to the production manager of Department B, not Department A.

AAT AQ2016 PRACTICE ASSESSMENT 1
ELEMENTS OF COSTING

Time allowed: 1 hour and 30 minutes

Elements of Costing
AAT practice assessment 1

Task 1 (10 marks)

(a) (i) Identify **TWO** examples of direct costs for a manufacturing business from the list below by dragging them into the answer box. **(2 marks)**

Direct costs	Rent	Production wages
	Raw materials	Administration wages
	Office telephone costs	Electricity for admin office

(ii) Complete the following sentences using the drop-down lists. **(2 marks)**

For manufacturing businesses raw materials are an example of a

[▼]

Picklist:

fixed cost
semi-variable cost
variable cost

For manufacturing businesses variable costs will [▼] with higher levels of activity.

Picklist:

increase
decrease

(b) (i) Identify whether the following statements are true or false. **(2 marks)**

Statement	True	False
For a service business the main purpose of financial accounts is to help management make decisions.		
Financial accounts include forecasts of future performance.		

(ii) **Complete the following sentence using the drop-down list.** **(1 mark)**

Financial accounting classifies costs by [▼]

Picklist:

behaviour
function
nature

Comfy & Co, a furniture manufacturer, uses a numeric coding system to allocate costs.

(c) (i) **Code the following transactions for the project, using the table below.** **(2 marks)**

Each transactions should have a four character code.

Activity	Code	Nature of cost	Sub-code	Transaction	Code
Materials	A	Direct	100	Wood used in production	
		Indirect	200	Wages for office staff	
Labour	B	Direct	100		
		Indirect	200		
Overheads	C	Direct	100		
		Indirect	200		

(ii) **Identify whether the following statement is true or false using the drop-down list below.** **(1 mark)**

An organisation's coding system MUST include both letters and numbers.

[▼]

Picklist:

True
False

Task 2 (10 marks)

(a) **Identify whether the following statements are true or false.**

(3 marks)

Statement	True	False
FIFO uses the most recent values of purchases to value closing inventory.		
LIFO assumes that the oldest items of inventory are issued first.		
AVCO values inventory issues based on the most recent purchase price.		

(b) **Identify the labour costing methods described below using the drop-down lists.** **(2 marks)**

Labour costs are calculated by multiplying a fixed rate by the hours worked:

[▼]

Labour costs are calculated by multiplying a fixed rate by the volume of items produced: [▼]

Picklist:

Piece rate
Time rate
Time rate with bonus

(c) **Identify TWO ways in which information on budgeted costs is used by clicking on the left-hand box and matching it to the appropriate right-hand boxes. You can remove a line by clicking on it.** **(2 marks)**

	To meet regulatory requirements
	For shareholders
Uses for budgeted costs	To calculate wages payable
	For planning and control
	To predict unit costs

(d) Complete the following sentences using the drop-down lists.

(3 marks)

The sales division of a business would be an example of [▼]

Picklist:

a cost centre
a profit centre
an investment centre

For a business division to be considered a profit centre it [▼] be responsible for capital expenditure.

Picklist:

should
should not

In manufacturing business that is largely automated the most appropriate overhead absorption method would be: [▼]

Picklist:

per labour hour
per machine hour
per unit

Task 3 (10 marks)

Argo Ltd uses the weighted average cost method (AVCO) to value its issues of materials to production.

A receipt and issue are shown in the inventory record below for material RM6.

(a) Complete the inventory record below for the issue of RM6 during January, and calculate the closing balance at 31 January.

The cost per kilogram (kg) entry should be completed in pounds (£) to THREE decimal places. **(6 marks)**

Inventory record – RM6

Date	Receipt			Issue			Balance	
	Quantity (kg)	Cost per kg (£)	Total cost (£)	Quantity (kg)	Cost per kg (£)	Total cost (£)	Quantity (kg)	Total cost (£)
1 January							1000	5800
12 January	1000	5.90	5900					
31 January				1680				

(b) **Complete the table below to show the cost of the issue on 31 January and closing inventory balance if Argo Ltd had instead used first in first out (FIFO) or last in first out (LIFO).**
(4 marks)

Method	Cost of issue on 31 January (£)	Closing inventory at 31 January (£)
FIFO		
LIFO		

Task 4 (8 marks)

All production workers in factory are paid a basic rate of £8 per hour.

Night shift workers are also paid an unsociable hours premium of 25% of basic pay. They are also paid for any overtime hour at the rate of basic rate + 20%.

There were six production workers in the night shift last month.

The factory sets a target for output each month. A bonus of £50 per worker is paid for each complete percent that actual output exceeds this target. Last month's target for the night shift was 35,000 units. The actual output, however, was 38,500 units.

Complete the table below to calculate the TOTAL labour cost of the night shift last month. **(8 marks)**

Labour cost for night shift	Hours	£
Basic pay	1,200	
Night shift unsociable hours premium		
Night shift overtime hours premium	200	
Totals before bonus payment		
Bonus payment		
Total cost including bonus		

Task 5 (10 marks)

Malborough Ltd is considering how to cost its products. It needs to decide on the overhead absorption basis it will use. The methods it is considering are:

- a machine hour basis
- a labour hour basis.

(a) **Complete the table below to show the two overhead absorption rates that Marlborough Ltd could use. Show your calculations to two decimal places.** **(2 marks)**

	Machine hour	Labour hour
Overheads (£)	450,000	450,000
Activity	30,000	56,250
Absorption rate (£)		

The following data relates to making one unit of one of its products:

Material: 5.0 kilograms (kg) at £3.20 per kg

Labour: 15 minutes at £15.40 per hour

Machine time: 10 minutes

(b) **Complete the table below (to two decimal places) to calculate the total unit cost, using each of the overhead absorption rates you calculated in (a).** **(8 marks)**

Cost	Machine hour (£)	Labour hour (£)
Material		
Labour		
Overheads		
Total unit cost		

....

Task 6 (10 marks)

(a) **Identify the type of cost of each of the three costs described below.** **(3 marks)**

Cost	Cost behaviour	Fixed	Variable	Semi-variable
Plant maintenance	£50,000 per year whatever the activity level + £2 per unit produced.			
Direct materials	£3.50 per unit produced.			
Depreciation of factory buildings	£60,000 per year.			

(b) **Complete the table to show the costs for production output levels of 2,000, 4,000 and 6,000 units.** **(7 marks)**

	2,000 units	4,000 units	6,000 units
Variable cost (£)	3,000		
Fixed cost (£)		15,000	
Total cost (£)			

Task 7 (8 marks)

A company has the following cost information for its last accounting period:

	£
Materials costs:	
Direct	20,000
Indirect	5,000
Labour costs:	
Direct	40,000
Indirect	25,000
Manufacturing expenses	70,000

Work in progress and finished goods inventories were as below:

	£
Work in progress:	
Opening	8,000
Closing	12,000
Finished goods:	
Opening	0
Closing	26,000

Complete the table below to show the company's cost structure for the last accounting period. **(8 marks)**

Cost structure for last accounting period	£
Prime cost	
Manufacturing overhead	
Total manufacturing cost	
Cost of goods manufactured	
Cost of goods sold	

Task 8 (14 marks)

Derwent Ltd uses the weighted average cost method (AVCO) to value its issues of materials to production.

The inventory record below shows its raw material received and issued to production for product PD6 in April.

(a) **Complete the inventory record below for the issue of this raw material during April and calculate the closing balance after this issue.**

The cost per kilogram (kg) entry should be completed in pounds (£) to THREE decimal places. (6 marks)

Raw material for PD6	Receipt			Issue			Balance	
Date	Quantity (kg)	Cost per kg (£)	Total cost (£)	Quantity (kg)	Cost per kg (£)	Total cost (£)	Quantity (kg)	Total cost (£)
1 April							5,000	20,000
8 April	10,000	4.75	47,500					
20 April				8,000				

(b) (i) **Calculate the total cost and cost per unit of April's production of PD6. (3 marks)**

　　(ii) **Calculate what these figures would have been if production had been only 40,000 units. (5 marks)**

Notes.

- The direct materials cost for the production of 50,000 units is your total cost figure calculated in part (a) above for the material issue.

- Show the cost per unit to three decimal places.

PD6 units produced and sold	50,000 £	40,000 £
Variable costs:		
Direct materials (see note above)		
Direct labour	42000	
Fixed costs:		
Manufacturing overheads	54000	
Total cost		
Cost per unit		

Task 9 (8 marks)

A profit centre of a furniture manufacturer experienced favourable variances on both sales and wages. The variance on sales was 10% of the budgeted figure, and the variance on wages was 5% of the budgeted figure.

(a) **Complete the table below to show the variance and the actual income and expense.** **(4 marks)**

	Budgeted income/expense £	Variance £	Adverse/ Favourable	Actual income/ expense achieved
Sales	29,250		Favourable	
Wages	23,100		Favourable	

You are reviewing the performance of the sales division.

(b) **Calculate the variance for selling and distribution overheads. Identify whether the variance is adverse or favourable by using the drop-down list below. Do not use a minus sign.**
(2 marks)

	Budgeted expense £	Actual expense incurred £	Variance £	Adverse/ Favourable
Selling and Distribution Overheads	43,300	39,500		▼

Picklist:

Adverse

Favourable

(c) **Identify whether the following statements are true or false.**

(2 marks)

Statement	True	False
A company that has an adverse variance on fixed overheads has spent less in that area than budgeted.		
Favourable variances always increase profits.		

Task 10 (12 marks)

(a) **Identify whether the following statement is true or false.**

(1 mark)

Statement	True	False
Adverse variances on sales are always considered to be significant.		

You have been asked to complete the performance report for the month. The budgeted and actual figures have already been summarised in the table below.

Company policy is that a significant variance must be:

- in excess of 10% of budget, and
- greater than £500.

Significant variances should be reported to the relevant manager for review and appropriate action.

(b) **Complete the table below to show each variance, the variance percentage as proportion of budget, and identify whether the variance is significant or not. Percentages should be to TWO decimal places.** **(6 marks)**

	Budgeted income/ expense £	Actual income/ expense incurred £	Variance £	Variance as percentage of budget %	Significant/not significant
Sales	29,250	42,175			▼
Wages	23,100	22,800			▼

Picklist:

Significant

Not Significant

You have been asked to provide information on the company's performance for the month.

- Variances in excess of 5% of budget, and that are greater than £500, are significant. They should be reported to the department manager.

- Adverse variances in excess of 20% of budget, and that are greater than £2,000, are significant. They should be reported to the department director.

The budgeted and actual figures have already been summarised in the table below.

	Budgeted £	Actual £
Sales	248,000	224,300

(c) **(i)** **Calculate the variance on sales.** **(1 mark)**

£ [ ]

(ii) **Calculate the percentage sales variance to TWO decimal places.** **(1 mark)**

[ ] %

(iii) **Identify whether the variance is favourable or adverse using the drop-down list.** **(1 mark)**

Picklist:

Favourable
Adverse

(iv) **Identify whether the variance is significant or not using the drop-down list.** **(1 mark)**

[▼]

Picklist:

Significant
Not significant

(v) **Identify who (if anyone) the variance should be reported to using the drop-down list.** **(1 mark)**

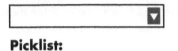

Picklist:

Department director
Department manager
Not required

AAT AQ2016 PRACTICE ASSESSMENT 1 ELEMENTS OF COSTING

ANSWERS

Elements of Costing
AAT practice assessment 1

Task 1 (10 marks)

(a) (i)   Identify TWO examples of direct costs for a manufacturing business from the list below by dragging them into the answer box.   (2 marks)

Direct costs	Rent	Production wages
Raw materials		
Production wages	Office telephone costs	Electricity for admin office

(ii) Complete the following sentences using the drop-down lists.   (2 marks)

For manufacturing businesses raw materials are an example of a variable cost. ▼

For manufacturing businesses variable costs will increase ▼ with higher levels of activity.

(b) (i)   Identify whether the following statements are true or false.   (2 marks)

Statement	True	False
For a service business the main purpose of financial accounts is to help management make decisions.		✓
Financial accounts include forecasts of future performance.		✓

(ii) Complete the following sentence using the drop-down list.   (1 mark)

Financial accounting classifies costs by function. ▼

97

(c) (i)   Code the following transactions for the project, using the table below. Each transaction should have a four character code.   (2 marks)

Activity	Code	Nature of cost	Sub-code	Transaction	Code
Materials	A	Direct	100	Wood used in production	A100
		Indirect	200	Wages for office staff	B200
Labour	B	Direct	100		
		Indirect	200		
Overheads	C	Direct	100		
		Indirect	200		

(ii)   Identify whether the following statement is true or false using the drop-down list below.   (1 mark)

An organisation's coding system MUST include both letters and numbers.

False ▼

....

Task 2 (10 marks)

(a)   Identify whether the following statements are true or false.
                                                                                     (3 marks)

Statement	True	False
FIFO uses the most recent values of purchases to value closing inventory.	✓	
LIFO assumes that the oldest items of inventory are issued first.		✓
AVCO values inventory issues based on the most recent purchase price.		✓

(b) **Identify the labour costing methods described below using the drop-down lists.** **(2 marks)**

Labour costs are calculated by multiplying a fixed rate by the hours worked:
Time rate ▼

Labour costs are calculated by multiplying a fixed rate by the volume of items produced: Piece rate ▼

(c) **Identify TWO ways in which information on budgeted costs is used by clicking on the left-hand box and matching it to the appropriate right-hand boxes. You can remove a line by clicking on it.** **(2 marks)**

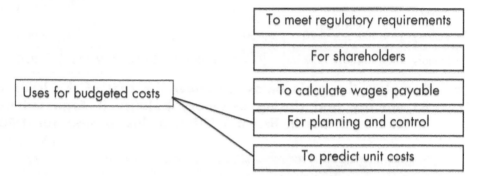

(d) **Complete the following sentences using the drop-down lists.** **(3 marks)**

The sales division of a business would be an example of a profit centre. ▼

For a business division to be considered a profit centre it should not ▼ be responsible for capital expenditure.

In manufacturing business that is largely automated the most appropriate overhead absorption method would be: per machine hour ▼

Task 3 (10 marks)

(a) Complete the inventory record below for the issue of RM6 during January, and calculate the closing balance at 31 January.

The cost per kilogram (kg) entry should be completed in pounds (£) to THREE decimal places. **(6 marks)**

Inventory record – RM6

Date	Receipt			Issue			Balance	
	Quantity (kg)	Cost per kg (£)	Total cost (£)	Quantity (kg)	Cost per kg (£)	Total cost (£)	Quantity (kg)	Total cost (£)
1 January							1,000	5,800
12 January	1,000	5.90	5,900				2,000	11,700
31 January				1,680	5.850	9,828	320	1,872

(b) Complete the table below to show the cost of the issue on 31 January and closing inventory balance if Argo Ltd had instead used first in first out (FIFO) or last in first out (LIFO). **(4 marks)**

Method	Cost of issue on 31 January (£)	Closing inventory at 31 January (£)
FIFO	9,812	1,888
LIFO	9,844	1,856

Task 4 (8 marks)

Complete the table below to calculate the TOTAL labour cost of the night shift last month. **(8 marks)**

Labour cost for night shift	Hours	£
Basic pay	1,200	9,600
Night shift unsociable hours premium		2,400
Night shift overtime hours premium	200	320
Totals before bonus payment	1,400	12,320
Bonus payment		3,000
Total cost including bonus		15,320

Task 5 (10 marks)

(a) **Complete the table below to show the two overhead absorption rates that Marlborough Ltd could use. Show your calculations to two decimal places.** **(2 marks)**

	Machine hour	Labour hour
Overheads (£)	450,000	450,000
Activity	30,000	56,250
Absorption rate (£)	15.00	8.00

(b) **Complete the table below (to two decimal places) to calculate the total unit cost, using each of the overhead absorption rates you calculated in (a).** **(8 marks)**

Cost	Machine hour (£)	Labour hour (£)
Material	16.00	16.00
Labour	3.85	3.85
Overheads	2.50	2.00
Total unit cost	22.35	21.85

Task 6 (10 marks)

(a) **Identify the type of cost of each of the three costs described below.** **(3 marks)**

Cost	Cost behaviour	Fixed	Variable	Semi-variable
Plant maintenance	£50,000 per year whatever the activity level + £2 per unit produced.			✓
Direct materials	£3.50 per unit produced.		✓	
Depreciation of factory buildings	£60,000 per year.	✓		

(b) Complete the table to show the costs for production output levels of 2,000, 4,000 and 6,000 units. **(7 marks)**

	2,000 units	4,000 units	6,000 units
Variable cost (£)	3,000	6,000	9,000
Fixed cost (£)	15,000	15,000	15,000
Total cost (£)	18,000	21,000	24,000

Task 7 (8 marks)

Complete the table below the company's cost structure for the last accounting period. **(8 marks)**

Cost structure for last accounting period	£
Prime cost	60,000
Manufacturing overhead	100,000
Total manufacturing cost	160,000
Cost of goods manufactured	156,000
Cost of goods sold	130,000

Task 8 (14 marks)

(a) Complete the inventory record below for the issue of this raw material during April and calculate the closing balance after this issue.

The cost per kilogram (kg) entry should be completed in pounds (£) to THREE decimal places. **(6 marks)**

Raw material for PD6	Receipt			Issue			Balance	
Date	Quantity (kg)	Cost per kg (£)	Total cost (£)	Quantity (kg)	Cost per kg (£)	Total cost (£)	Quantity (kg)	Total cost (£)
1 April							5,000	20,000
8 April	10,000	4.75	47,500				15,000	67,500
20 April				8,000	4.500	36,000	7,000	31,500

(b) **(i)** Calculate the total cost and cost per unit of April's production of PD6. **(3 marks)**

(ii) Calculate what these figures would have been if production had been only 40,000 units. **(5 marks)**

Notes.

- The direct materials cost for the production of 50,000 units is your total cost figure calculated in part (a) above for the material issue.

- Show the cost per unit to three decimal places.

PD6 units produced and sold	50,000 £	40,000 £
Variable costs:		
Direct materials (see note above)	36,000	28,800
Direct labour	42,000	33,600
Fixed costs:		
Manufacturing overheads	54,000	54,000
Total cost	132,000	116,400
Cost per unit	2.640	2.910

Task 9 (8 marks)

(a) Complete the table below to show the variance and the actual income and expense. **(4 marks)**

	Budgeted income/expense £	Variance £	Adverse/ Favourable	Actual income/ expense achieved
Sales	29,250	2,925	Favourable	32,175
Wages	23,100	1,155	Favourable	21,945

You are reviewing the performance of the sales division.

(b) Calculate the variance for selling and distribution overheads. Identify whether the variance is adverse or favourable by using drop-down list below. Do not use a minus sign.

(2 marks)

	Budgeted expense £	Actual expense incurred £	Variance £	Adverse/ Favourable
Selling and Distribution Overheads	43,300	39,500	3,800	Favourable ▼

(c) Identify whether the following statements are true or false.

(2 marks)

Statement	True	False
A company that has an adverse variance on fixed overheads has spent less in that area than budgeted.		✓
Favourable variances always increase profits.	✓	

Task 10 (12 marks)

(a) Identify whether the following statement is true or false.

(1 mark)

Statement	True	False
Adverse variances on sales are always considered to be significant.		✓

(b) Complete the table below to show each variance, the variance percentage as proportion of budget, and identify whether the variance is significant or not. Percentages should be to TWO decimal places.

(6 marks)

	Budgeted income/ expense £	Actual income/ expense incurred £	Variance £	Variance as percentage of budget £	Significant/not significant
Sales	29,250	42,175	12,925	44.19	Significant ▼
Wages	23,100	22,800	300	1.30	Not significant ▼

(c) **(i)** **Calculate the variance on sales.** **(1 mark)**

£	23,700

(ii) **Calculate the percentage sales variance to TWO decimal places.** **(1 mark)**

9.56	%

(iii) **Identify whether the variance is favourable or adverse using the drop-down list.** **(1 mark)**

Adverse ▼

(iv) **Identify whether the variance is significant or not using the drop-down list.** **(1 mark)**

Significant ▼

(v) **Identify who (if anyone) the variance should be reported to using the drop-down list.** **(1 mark)**

Department manager ▼

AAT AQ2016 PRACTICE ASSESSMENT 2 ELEMENTS OF COSTING

You are advised to attempt practice assessment 2 online from the AAT website. This will ensure you are prepared for how the assessment will be presented on the AAT's system when you attempt the real assessment. Please access the assessment using the address below:

https://www.aat.org.uk/training/study-support/search

BPP PRACTICE ASSESSMENT 1
ELEMENTS OF COSTING

Time allowed: 1.5 hours

Elements of Costing
BPP practice assessment 1

Task 1 (8 marks)

Management use costing techniques to help them with planning, control and decision making.

(a) **Indicate whether the following statements are true or false by ticking the relevant boxes in the table below.** **(4 marks)**

Statement	True	False
The fixed cost per unit rises as the level of output rises.		
The variable cost per unit falls as the level of output rises		
LIFO gives the lowest value of closing inventory if general prices are rising.		
An investment centre can have capital amounts coded to it.		

The table below lists some of the characteristics of financial accounting and cost accounting.

(b) **Indicate the characteristics for each system by ticking the relevant boxes in the table below.** **(4 marks)**

Characteristic	Financial accounting	Cost accounting
The statements of this system are used by lenders and suppliers of credit to the business to assess whether they will get paid.		
Information from this system is used for planning, control and decision making.		
There is no legal requirement for the format of this system's statements.		
This system incorporates non-monetary measures such as quantities.		

Task 2 (8 marks)

Pizzia Ltd is a fast food restaurant.

(a) **Classify the following costs it incurred by behaviour (fixed, variable or semi-variable overhead) by ticking the relevant boxes in the table below.** **(4 marks)**

Cost	Variable	Fixed	Semi-variable
Restaurant lighting costs consisting of a fixed and usage charge.			
Salary of restaurant manager.			
Flour purchased for making pizzas.			
Wages of pizza maker paid on a piecework basis.			

Kilnsey Ltd is in business as a walking boot shop selling boots and making repairs.

(b) **Classify the following costs incurred by nature (direct or indirect) by ticking the relevant boxes in the table below.** **(4 marks)**

Cost	Direct	Indirect
Wages of cobbler employed to repair the boots		
Rent and rates for shop and workshop		
Licences paid per item to boot suppliers to stock their boots		
Oil for stitching machine		

BPP
LEARNING MEDIA

Task 3 (12 marks)

Dales Ltd has set up an investment centre for a restaurant project it is undertaking over a period of months. It uses an alpha coding system for its investments, revenues and costs and then further classifies numerically as outlined in the table below.

Code the following transactions for the project, using the table below.

Each transaction should have a five character code.

Activity	Code	Nature of cost	Sub-code	Transaction	Code
Investments	IV	External	100	Solicitor fees for arranging bar licence.	
		Internal	200	Bar sales.	
Revenues	RE	Restaurant	100	Fresh vegetables bought in daily from local farmers.	
		Bar	200	Waiting staff salaries.	
Costs	CO	Material	100	Loan used to set up restaurant and bar.	
		Labour	200	Security manager salary.	
		Overheads	300		

Task 4 (8 marks)

(a) **Identify the type of cost behaviour (fixed, variable or semi-variable) described in each statement by ticking the relevant boxes in the table below.** (3 marks)

Statement	Fixed	Variable	Semi-variable
At 4,000 units, this cost is £6.25 per unit and at 5,000 units, it is £5.00 per unit.			
At 12,000 units, this cost is £90,000 and at 14,000 units, this cost is £105,000.			
At 5,000 units, this cost is £26,000 and at 8,000 units, it is £35,000.			

(b) **Complete the table below by inserting all costs for the activity levels of 2,000 and 8,000.** (5 marks)

	2,000 units	4,500 units	7,500 units	8,000 units
Variable cost (£)				
Fixed cost (£)				
Total cost (£)		23,750	34,250	

Task 5 (14 marks)

Munchcin Ltd wants to calculate the unit cost for one of its products. It needs to calculate an overhead absorption rate to apply to each unit. It is considering one of the following methods:

- Per machine hour
- Per labour hour
- Per unit

Total factory activity is forecast as follows:

Machine hours	40,000
Labour hours	32,000
Units	50,000
Overheads	£800,000

(a) **Complete the table below to show the possible overhead absorption rates that Munchcin Ltd could use. The absorption rates should be calculated to two decimal places.**   **(6 marks)**

	Machine hour	Labour hour	Unit
Overheads (£)	800,000	800,000	800,000
Activity			
Absorption rate (£)			

The following data relates to making one unit of the product:

Material	5 kilos at £12 per kilo
Labour	30 minutes at £48 per hour
Production time	45 minutes

(b) **Complete the table below (to two decimal places) to calculate the total unit cost, using the three overhead absorption rates you have calculated in (a).**   **(8 marks)**

Cost	Machine hour £	Labour hour £	Unit £
Material			
Labour			
Direct cost			
Overheads			
Total unit cost			

Task 6 (12 marks)

Florrie Ltd wish to know how fixed costs, variable costs, total costs and unit cost behave at different levels of production.

Fixed costs are £24,000 and variable costs are £3.30 per unit.

Complete the table below. Unit costs should be calculated to two decimal places.

Units	Fixed costs £	Variable costs £	Total costs £	Unit cost £
3,000				
6,000				
12,000				

Task 7 (12 marks)

You are told the opening inventory of a single raw material in the stores is 6,300 units at £2.70 per unit. During the month, 5,100 units at £2.80 per unit are received and the following week 9,600 units are issued.

(a) **Identify the valuation method by dragging the statements into the correct column below.** **(3 marks)**

FIFO	LIFO	AVCO

Statements:

The closing inventory is valued at £4,860.	The closing inventory is valued at £5,040.

The issue of 9,600 units is costed at £26,349.

(b) **Identify whether the following statements are true or false.** **(3 marks)**

Statement	True	False
AVCO values the closing inventory at £5,040		
LIFO costs the issue of 9,600 units at £26,430		
FIFO costs the issue of 9,600 units at £26,250		

Ripon Ltd has the following movements in a certain type of inventory into and out of its stores for the month of October:

Date	Receipts		Issues	
	Units	Cost £	Units	Cost £
October 5	300	900		
October 8	600	2,400		
October 12	500	2,500		
October 18			1,200	
October 25	1,000	6,000		

(c)   **Complete the table below by entering the cost of issues and closing inventory values.**   **(6 marks)**

Method	Cost of issue on October 18 £	Closing inventory at October 31 £
FIFO		
LIFO		
AVCO		

Task 8 (10 marks)

An employee is paid £20 an hour and is expected to make 25 units an hour.

For any excess production, the employee will be paid a bonus of 45p per unit.

(a)   **Identify whether the following statement is true or false by ticking the relevant boxes in the table below.**   **(1 mark)**

Statement	True	False
During a 35-hour week the employee produces 875 units and earns total pay of £700.		

Settle Ltd pays a time-rate of £10 per hour to its direct labour for a standard 37.5-hour week. Any of the labour force working in excess of 37.5 hours is paid an overtime rate of £12 per hour.

(b)   **Calculate the basic wage, overtime and gross wage for the week for the two employees in the table below.**   **(6 marks)**

Note. If no overtime is paid, you should enter 0 as the overtime for that employee.

Employee	Hours worked	Basic wage £	Overtime £	Gross wage £
N Crane	37.5			
F Crane	39			

Joycey Ltd wishes to pay its employees using either the time-rate method with bonus, or the piecework method. The time-rate used is £11.75 per hour and an employee is expected to produce 10 units per hour, and anything over this paid a bonus of £0.90 per unit. The piecework payment rate is £1.10 per unit.

(c) **Complete the table below for the two methods, showing the gross wage for the time-rate with bonus and the piecework wage.** (3 marks)

Note. **If no bonus is paid, you should enter 0 as the bonus for that employee in the table.**

Hours worked	Unit output	Basic wage £	Bonus £	Gross wage £	Piecework wage £
36	590				

Task 9 (8 marks)

A number of statements about variances are set out in the table below.

(a) **Identify whether the following statements are true or false.**
(4 marks)

Statement	
If budgeted sales are 7,000 units at £20.50 per unit and actual sales are £144,000, the sales variance is favourable.	▼
A favourable cost variance occurs when an actual cost of £5,800 is compared to a budgeted cost of £15 per unit for a budgeted output of 390 units.	▼
Variances can be expressed as a percentage of the budgeted amount to determine the significance	▼
A variance arises from a comparison of actual costs from a past period with budgeted costs of a future period.	▼

Picklist:

True
False

Jaitinder has produced a performance report detailing budgeted and actual costs for last month.

(b) **In the table below, determine whether the variance for each cost type is adverse or favourable.** **(4 marks)**

Cost type	Budget £	Actual £	
Direct material	83,950	84,050	▼
Direct labour	63,290	63,250	▼
Production overheads	84,750	84,850	▼
Administration overheads	36,320	36,290	▼

Picklist:

Adverse
Favourable

Task 10 (8 marks)

Trane Ltd requires a performance report detailing budgeted data, actual data and variances for last month.

Budgeted data for the month Included:

Sales	5,200 units at £40 per unit
Material	4,300 kilos at £15 per kilo
Labour	3,750 hours at £25 per hour
Overheads	£128,000

In the table below, insert the budget amount for each item and calculate the variances.

Item	Budget £	Actual £	Variance £
Sales		205,400	
Material		64,800	
Labour		92,700	
Overheads		127,800	

BPP PRACTICE ASSESSMENT 1
ELEMENTS OF COSTING

ANSWERS

Elements of Costing
BPP practice assessment 1

Task 1

(a)

	True	False
The fixed cost per unit rises as the level of output rises		✓
The variable cost per unit falls as the level of output rises		✓
LIFO gives the lowest value of closing inventory if general prices are rising	✓	
An investment centre can have capital amounts coded to it	✓	

(b)

Characteristic	Financial accounting	Cost accounting
The statements of this system are used by lenders and suppliers of credit to the business to assess whether they will get paid.	✓	
Information from this system is used for planning, control and decision making.		✓
There is no legal requirement for the format of this system's statements.		✓
This system incorporates non-monetary measures such as quantities.		✓

Task 2

(a)

Cost	Variable	Fixed	Semi-variable
Restaurant lighting costs consisting of a fixed and usage charge.			✓
Salary of restaurant manager.		✓	
Flour purchased for making pizzas.	✓		
Wages of pizza maker paid on a piecework basis.	✓		

(b)

Cost	Direct	Indirect
Wages of cobbler employed to repair the boots	✓	
Rent and rates for shop and workshop		✓
Licences paid per item to boot suppliers to stock their boots	✓	
Oil for stitching machine		✓

Task 3

Activity	Code	Nature of cost	Sub-code	Transaction	Code
Investments	IV	External	100	Solicitor fees for arranging bar licence.	CO300
		Internal	200	Bar sales.	RE200
Revenues	RE	Restaurant	100	Fresh vegetables bought in daily from local farmers.	CO100
		Bar	200	Waiting staff salaries.	CO200
Costs	CO	Material	100	Loan used to set up restaurant and bar.	IN100
		Labour	200	Security manager salary.	CO200
		Overheads	300		

Task 4

(a)

Statement	Fixed	Variable	Semi-variable
At 4,000 units, this cost is £6.25 per unit and at 5,000 units, it is £5.00 per unit.	✔		
At 12,000 units, this cost is £90,000 and at 14,000 units, this cost is £105,000.		✔	
At 5,000 units, this cost is £26,000 and at 8,000 units, it is £35,000.			✔

(b)

	2,000 units	4,500 units	7,500 units	8,000 units
Variable cost (£)	7,000			28,000
Fixed cost (£)	8,000			8,000
Total cost (£)	15,000	23,750	34,250	36,000

Workings

Variable cost per unit = (£34,250 – £23,750)/(7,500 – 4,500) = £3.50 per unit
Fixed cost = £34,250 – (7,500 × £3.50) = £8,000
Variable cost of 2,000 units = (2,000 × £3.50) = £7,000
Variable cost of 8,000 units = (8,000 × £3.50) = £28,000

Task 5

(a)

	Machine hour	Labour hour	Unit
Overheads (£)	800,000	800,000	800,000
Activity	40,000	32,000	50,000
Absorption rate (£)	20.00	25.00	16.00

(b)

Cost	Machine hour £	Labour hour £	Unit £
Material	60.00	60.00	60.00
Labour	24.00	24.00	24.00
Direct cost	84.00	84.00	84.00
Overheads	15.00	12.50	16.00
Total unit cost	99.00	96.50	100.00

Workings

Material = 5 kilos × £12 = £60.00
Labour = (30/60) hours × £48 = £24.00
Direct cost = material + labour = £60.00 + £24.00 = £84.00
Overheads based on machine hours = (45/60) hours × £20 = £15.00
Overheads based on labour hours = (30/60) hours × £25.00 = £12.50
Overheads based on number of units = 1 × £16.00 = £16.00

Task 6

Units	Fixed costs £	Variable costs £	Total costs £	Unit cost £
3,000	24,000	9,900	33,900	11.30
6,000	24,000	19,800	43,800	7.30
12,000	24,000	39,600	63,600	5.30

Task 7

(a)

FIFO	LIFO	AVCO
The closing inventory is valued at £5,040.	The closing inventory is valued at £4,860.	The issue of 9,600 units is costed at £26,349.

(b)

Statement	True	False
AVCO values the closing inventory at £5,040.		✓
LIFO costs the issue of 9,600 units at £26,430	✓	
FIFO costs the issue of 9,600 units at £26,250.	✓	

Workings

	Units	Per unit £	Total £	Balance £
Opening inventory	6,300	2.70	17,010	17,010
Received	5,100	2.80	14,280	31,290
	11,400			
Issued	(9,600)			
Closing inventory	1,800			

	FIFO	LIFO	AVCO
Issue	£17,010 + (3,300 × £2.80) = £26,250	£14,280 + (4,500 × £2.70) = £26,430	9,600 × £31,290/11,400 = £26,349
Closing inventory	1,800 × £2.80 = £5,040	1,800 × £2.70 = £4,860	1,800 × £31,290/11,400 = £4,941

(c)

Method	Cost of issue on 18 October £	Closing inventory at 31 October £
FIFO	(900 + 2,400 + (300/500 × 2,500)) = **£4,800**	(6,000 + (200/500 × 2,500)) = **£7,000**
LIFO	(2,500 + 2,400 + (100/300 × 900)) = **£5,200**	(6,000 + (200/300 × 900)) = **£6,600**
AVCO	(1,200/1,400 × 5,800) = **£4,971**	(6,000 + (200/1,400 × 5,800)) = **£6,829**

Task 8

(a)

Statement	True	False
During a 35-hour week the employee produces 875 units and earns total pay of £700.	✓	

(b)

Employee	Hours worked	Basic wage £	Overtime £	Gross wage £
N Crane	37.5	375.00	0	375.00
F Crane	39	375.00	18.00	393.00

(c)

Hours worked	Unit output	Basic wage £	Bonus £	Gross wage £	Piecework wage £
36	590	(36 × £11.75) 423	((590 – 360) × £0.90) 207	630	(590 × £1.10) 649

Task 9

(a)

Statement	
If budgeted sales are 7,000 units at £20.50 per unit and actual sales are £144,000, the sales variance is favourable.	True
A favourable cost variance occurs when an actual cost of £5,800 is compared to a budgeted cost of £15 per unit for a budgeted output of 390 units.	True
Variances can be expressed as a percentage of the budgeted amount to determine the significance	True
A variance arises from a comparison of actual costs from a past period with budgeted costs of a future period.	False

(b)

Cost type	Budget £	Actual £		
Direct material	83,950	84,050	Adverse	▼
Direct labour	63,290	63,250	Favourable	▼
Production overheads	84,750	84,850	Adverse	▼
Administration overheads	36,320	36,290	Favourable	▼

Task 10

Item	Budget £	Actual £	Variance £
Sales	208,000	205,400	2,600
Material	64,500	64,800	300
Labour	93,750	92,700	1,050
Overheads	128,000	127,800	200

BPP PRACTICE ASSESSMENT 2
ELEMENTS OF COSTING

Time allowed: 1.5 hours

Elements of Costing
BPP practice assessment 2

Task 1 (8 marks)

(a) Costing uses a number of techniques to assist management.

Identify the following statements as being True or False by putting a tick in the relevant column of the table below.

(5 marks)

Statement	True	False
When a time-rate system is used to pay employees, pay remains the same even when output fluctuates due to demand		
All variances between budget and actual costs and income should be treated as significant and be fully investigated		
When a piecework system of pay is used, less efficient workers are paid the same as more efficient ones		
An adverse variance means budgeted costs are lower than actual costs		
AVCO costs issues of inventory at the oldest purchase price		

(b) The table below lists some of the characteristics of manufacturing, retail and service organisations.

Indicate a characteristic for each organisation by putting a tick in the relevant column of the table below. **(3 marks)**

Characteristic	Retail	Manufacturing	Service
Does not make or sell a physical product			
Buys in ready-made goods to sell			
Buys in raw materials			

Task 2 (8 marks)

(a) Exmouth Ltd is a manufacturer of tweed cloth.

Classify the following costs by their behaviour (fixed, variable, or semi-variable) by putting a tick in the relevant column of the table below. (4 marks)

Cost	Fixed	Variable	Semi-variable
Labour costs paid on a piecework basis			
Spun wool used in making the cloth			
Marketing cost for the year			
Telephone costs for the sales staff that include a standing charge			

(b) Totnes Ltd is in business as a beauty salon.

Classify the following costs by nature (direct or indirect) by putting a tick in the relevant column of the table below.
(4 marks)

Cost	Direct	Indirect
Wages of beauticians		
Wages of security guard		
Rent and rates for salon		
Nail polish used on nails		

Task 3 (10 marks)

Torbay Limited offers two services for dogs: kennel care and dog grooming. It uses a numeric coding system for its one profit centre (sales) and three cost centres (operations, administration, and distribution) as outlined in the table below. Each code has a sub-code so each transaction will be coded as **/***.

Element of cost	Cost code	Sub-classification	Sub-code
Sales	10	Kennel care	100
		Grooming	200
Operations	30	Direct cost	100
		Indirect cost	200
Administration	50	Direct cost	100
		Indirect cost	200
Distribution	70	Direct cost	100
		Indirect cost	200

You are required to classify the income and expense transactions shown in the transaction column of the table below using the code column for your answer.

Transaction	Code
Shampoo used in grooming	
Fees for solicitors to negotiate rent reduction on parlour	
Wages of kennel maid	
Wages of delivery driver	
Fees received for keeping dogs in kennels	

Task 4 (8 marks)

(a) **Identify the following statements as either True or False by putting a tick in the relevant column of the table below.**

(3 marks)

Statement	True	False
Fixed costs never change		
Variable costs change with output levels		
Semi-variable costs show a step increase at a particular level of output		

(b) Plustyre Ltd fixes cars and makes sure they are valeted so they are returned to their owners in a perfect state.

Classify the following costs as either fixed or variable by putting a tick in the relevant column of the table below.

(4 marks)

Costs	Fixed	Variable
Valets paid at piecework rate for each car valeted		
Hourly wages of mechanics paid for each car fixed		
Salaries of supervisors		
Rent for the workshop used to fix cars		

(c) Kingswear Ltd has budgeted factory overheads for the next period of £60,000 and budgeted factory machine hours of 40,000 hours.

What is the overhead absorption rate per machine hour?

(1 mark)

£	

Task 5 (12 marks)

Yellow Trees Ltd makes a product called the Kween and for a production level of 20,000 units has the following cost details:

Materials   5,000 kilos at £10 per kilo
Labour   4,000 hours at £15 an hour
Machine   40,000 hours

The overhead absorption rate per machine hour is £1.25.

(a)   Complete the table below to show the unit product cost at the production level of 20,000 units.   (4 marks)

Element	Unit product cost £
Material	
Labour	
Direct cost	
Overheads	
Total	

Yellow Tree's managers wish to know how fixed costs, variable costs, total costs and unit cost behave at different levels of production.

You are told that fixed costs are £58,000 and variable costs are £3.20 per unit.

(b)   Complete the table below. Unit costs should be calculated to two decimal places.   (8 marks)

Units	Fixed costs £	Variable costs £	Total costs £	Unit cost £
8,000				
10,000				
20,000				

Task 6 (12 marks)

You are told the opening inventory of a good purchased for resale is 1,500 units at £9 per unit. In week 2 of the month further purchases were made of 1,000 at £10 per unit. In week 3, 500 units were issued from stores.

(a) **Identify the valuation method described in the statements below.** (3 marks)

Characteristic	FIFO	LIFO	AVCO
The issue of 500 units is costed at £5,000			
Closing inventory is valued at £18,800			
Closing inventory is valued at £19,000			

(b) **Identify whether each of the following statements is True or False by putting a tick in the relevant column.** (3 marks)

Statement	True	False
AVCO values the issue at £4,700		
FIFO costs the issue at £4,800		
LIFO values the closing inventory at £18,500		

Jersey Ltd has the following movements in a certain type of inventory into and out of its stores for the month of May:

Date	Receipts Units	Cost	Issues Units	Cost
May 5	500	£1,500		
May 8	750	£3,000		
May 12	1,250	£6,250		
May 18			1,500	
May 25	1,000	£6,000		

(c) **Complete the table below for the issue and closing inventory values.** **(6 marks)**

Method	Cost of issue on 18 May £	Closing inventory at 31 May £
FIFO		
LIFO		
AVCO		

Task 7 (12 marks)

(a) **Identify whether each of the following statements describes the time-rate method of paying employees by putting a tick in the relevant column.** **(3 marks)**

Payment method	Time-rate method	NOT time-rate method
An amount is paid to the employee for each unit or task successfully completed		
A basic amount is paid per hour worked		
If output exceeds a preset level an incentive is paid in addition to basic pay		

(b) Cardiff Ltd pays a time-rate of £15 per hour to its direct labour for a standard 35-hour week. Any of the labour force working in excess of 35 hours is paid an overtime rate of £25 per hour.

Calculate the gross wage for the week for the two workers in the table below. **(6 marks)**

Note. **If no overtime is paid you should enter 0 as the overtime for that worker.**

Worker	Hours worked	Basic wage £	Overtime £	Gross wage £
J Edwards	35 hours			
L Rakowski	41 hours			

Swansea Ltd uses a piecework method to pay labour in one of its factories. The rate used is 70p per unit produced.

(c) **Calculate the gross wage for the week for the two workers in the table below.** **(3 marks)**

Worker	Units produced in week	Gross wage £
G Gently	350 units	
B Flemming	370 units	
A Ransome	390 units	

Task 8 (12 marks)

Torre Ltd has the following actual results for the month of November, which it wishes to compare with the November budget.

Income   £80,000

Costs
Materials   £15,000
Labour   £25,000
Overheads   £12,000

Enter the above data into the table below, calculate the variance for each item of income and cost, and determine indicate whether it is adverse of favourable using the picklist.

	Budget £	Actual £	Variance £	Adverse or favourable
Income	78,500			
Materials	16,000			
Labour	23,200			
Overheads	10,000			

Picklist:

Adverse
Favourable

Task 9 (10 marks)

Wills Ltd has produced a table detailing budgeted costs for last month. Actual results were as follows:

Materials	10,000 kgs at £2.62 per kg
Labour	£73,125
Production overheads	£15,120
Administration overheads	£21,950
Selling and Distribution overheads	£24,950

Enter the above data into the table below and calculate the amount of each variance.

Expenditure	Budget £	Actual £	Variance £
Materials	25,500		
Labour	57,000		
Production overheads	18,000		
Administration overheads	22,000		
Selling and Distribution overheads	23,000		

Task 10 (8 marks)

The managers of Jayl Ltd require the budget report below for last month to be completed. In particular, they want production cost variances expressed as a percentage of budget.

Actual costs were:

Direct material	£123,400
Direct labour	£129,200
Production overheads	£136,700

(a) **Calculate the production cost variances and the variances as a percentage of budget, rounded to two decimal places.**

(6 marks)

Cost	Budget £	Variance £	Variance %
Direct material	131,800		
Direct labour	143,812		
Production overheads	125,000		

The following table shows budgeted costs plus variances for last month for Dahl Ltd. It is company policy to provide managers with a variance report highlighting significant variances, which is any variance of 10% or more

(b) **Indicate whether each variance is significant or not significant by using the picklist.** **(2 marks)**

Cost	Budget £	Variance £	Adverse/ Favourable	Significant/ Not significant
Administration overheads	54,000	5,980	Adverse	
Selling and distribution overheads	42,000	1,150	Adverse	

Picklist:

Significant
Not significant

BPP PRACTICE ASSESSMENT 2
ELEMENTS OF COSTING

ANSWERS

Elements of Costing
BPP practice assessment 2

Task 1

(a)

Statement	True	False
When a time-rate system is used to pay employees, pay remains the same even when output fluctuates due to demand	✓	
All variances between budget and actual costs and income should be treated as significant and be fully investigated		✓
When a piecework system of pay is used, less efficient workers are paid the same as more efficient ones		✓
An adverse variance means budgeted costs are lower than actual costs	✓	
AVCO costs issues of inventory at the oldest purchase price		✓

(b)

Characteristic	Retail	Manufacturing	Service
Does not make or sell a physical product			✓
Buys in ready-made goods to sell	✓		
Buys in raw materials		✓	

Task 2

(a)

Cost	Fixed	Variable	Semi-variable
Labour costs paid on a piecework basis		✓	
Spun wool used in making the cloth		✓	
Marketing cost for the year	✓		
Telephone costs for the sales staff that include a standing charge			✓

(b)

Cost	Direct	Indirect
Wages of beauticians	✓	
Wages of security guard		✓
Rent and rates for salon		✓
Nail polish used on nails	✓	

Task 3

Transaction	Code
Shampoo used in grooming	30/100
Fees for solicitors to negotiate rent reduction on parlour	50/200
Wages of kennel maid	30/100
Wages of delivery driver	70/200
Fees received for keeping dogs in kennels	10/100

Task 4

(a)

Statement	True	False
Fixed costs never change		✓
Variable costs change with output levels	✓	
Semi-variable costs show a step increase at a particular level of output		✓

(b)

Costs	Fixed	Variable
Valets paid at piecework rate for each car valeted		✓
Hourly wages of mechanics paid for each car fixed		✓
Salaries of supervisors	✓	
Rent for the workshop used to fix cars	✓	

(c) £60,000/40,000 hours = £1.50 per hour

Task 5

(a)

Element	Unit product cost £
Material	2.50
Labour	3.00
Direct cost	5.50
Overheads	2.50
Total	8.00

Workings

Material cost per unit = (5,000 × £10)/20,000 = £2.50
Labour cost per unit = (4,000 × £15)/20,000 = £3.00
Overheads per unit = (40,000 × £1.25)/20,000 = £2.50

(b)

Units	Fixed costs £	Variable costs £	Total costs £	Unit cost £
8,000	58,000	25,600	83,600	10.45
10,000	58,000	32,000	90,000	9.00
20,000	58,000	64,000	122,000	6.10

Task 6

(a)

Characteristic	FIFO	LIFO	AVCO
The issue of 500 units is costed at £5,000		✓	
Closing inventory is valued at £18,800			✓
Closing inventory is valued at £19,000	✓		

(b)

Statement	True	False
AVCO values the issue at £4,700	✓	
FIFO costs the issue at £4,800		✓
LIFO values the closing inventory at £18,500	✓	

Workings

	Units	Per unit £	Total £	Balance £
Opening inventory	1,500	9	13,500	13,500
Received	1,000	10	10,000	23,500
	2,500			
Issued	(500)			
Closing inventory	2,000			

	FIFO	LIFO	AVCO
Issue	500 × £9 = £4,500	500 × £10 = £5,000	500 × £23,500/2,500 = £4,700
Inventory	(1,000 × £9) + (1,000 × £10) = £19,000	(1,500 × £9) + (500 × £10) = £18,500	2,000 × £23,500/2,500 = £18,800

(c)

Method	Cost of issue on 18 May	Closing inventory at 31 May
FIFO	1,500 + 3,000 + (250/1,250 × 6,250) = **£5,750**	6,000 + (1,000/1,250 × 6,250) = **£11,000**
LIFO	6,250 + (250/750 × 3,000) = **£7,250**	1,500 + (500/750 × 3,000) + 6,000 = **£9,500**
AVCO	[(1,500 + 3,000 + 6,250)/2,500] × 1,500 = **£6,450**	[(1,500 + 3,000 + 6,250)/2,500] × 1,000 + 6,000 = **£10,300**

Task 7

(a)

Payment method	Time-rate method	NOT time-rate method
An amount is paid to the employee for each unit or task successfully completed		✓
A basic amount is paid per hour worked	✓	
If output exceeds a preset level an incentive is paid in addition to basic pay		✓

(b)

Worker	Hours worked	Basic wage £	Overtime £	Gross wage £
J Edwards	35 hours	525	0	525
L Rakowski	41 hours	525	150	675

(c)

Worker	Units produced in week	Gross wage £
G Gently	350 units	245 (350 x £0.70)
B Flemming	370 units	259 (370 x £0.70)
A Ransome	390 units	273 (390 x £0.70)

Task 8

	Budget £	Actual £	Variance £	Adverse or Favourable
Income	78,500	80,000	1,500	Favourable
Materials	16,000	15,000	1,000	Favourable
Labour	23,200	25,000	1,800	Adverse
Overheads	10,000	12,000	2,000	Adverse

Task 9

Expenditure	Budget £	Actual £	Variance £
Materials	25,500	26,200	700
Labour	57,000	73,125	16,125
Production overheads	18,000	15,120	2,880
Administration overheads	22,000	21,950	50
Selling and Distribution overheads	23,000	24,950	1,950

Task 10

(a)

Cost	Budget £	Variance £	Variance %
Direct material	131,800	8,400	6.37
Direct labour	143,812	14,612	10.16
Production overheads	125,000	11,700	9.36

(b)

Cost	Budget £	Variance £	Adverse/ Favourable	Significant/ Not significant
Administration overheads	54,000	5,980	Adverse	Significant
Selling and distribution overheads	42,000	1,150	Adverse	Not significant

BPP PRACTICE ASSESSMENT 3 ELEMENTS OF COSTING

Time allowed: 1.5 hours

Elements of Costing
BPP practice assessment 3

Task 1 (8 marks)

(a) **Identify whether the following statements are True or False by putting a tick in the relevant column of the table below.**

(4 marks)

Statement	True	False
If prices of materials are rising FIFO will give a higher inventory valuation than LIFO		
A variance is the difference between budgeted and expected cost		
In a LIFO system the most recent purchases are assumed to have been issued first		
Financial accounting results in the presentation of financial information for external users		

(b) The table below lists some typical business transactions.

Indicate whether each one is capital or revenue by putting a tick in the relevant column. **(4 marks)**

Transaction	Capital	Revenue
Purchase of office furniture for office manager		
Purchase of office furniture by office furniture saleroom for resale		
Paying VAT		
Making cash sales		

Task 2 (8 marks)

(a) Derwentwater Ltd makes dinghies.

Classify the following costs by function (production, administration, selling and distribution or finance) by putting a tick in the relevant column of the table below. (4 marks)

Cost	Production	Administration	Selling and distribution	Finance
Advertising dinghies in local newspaper				
Material for making sails in the factory				
Fees to estate agent for locating new premises				
Interest charged on long-term loan				

(b) Bassenthwaite Ltd is a pottery making bowls and cups.

Classify the following costs by their behaviour (fixed, variable, or semi-variable) by putting a tick in the relevant column of the table below. **(4 marks)**

Cost	Fixed	Variable	Semi-variable
Charge for electricity for the kilns firing the pots that includes a standing charge			
Annual entertainment budget for the pottery			
Cost of glazes bought in to glaze the pots			
Labour costs for potters paid on a piecework basis			

Task 3 (10 marks)

Cockermouth Limited operates three cost centres: two bakeries and a head office/distribution centre. It uses an alpha-numeric coding system for its cost centres and then further classifies each element by nature (direct or indirect cost) as below. So, for example, the code for materials used in Bakery 2 is 2DIR.

Cost centre	Code	Nature of cost	Code
Bakery 1	1	Direct	DIR
		Indirect	IND
Bakery 2	2	Direct	DIR
		Indirect	IND
Head office/distribution centre	3	Direct	DIR
		Indirect	IND

Code the following costs, extracted from invoices and the payroll, using the table below.

Cost	Code
Wages of delivery driver	
Fees for annual audit by local accountants	
Yeast used in baking at Bakery 1	
Bakers' salaries at Bakery 2	
Power used at Bakery 1	

Task 4 (8 marks)

(a) Identify the following statements as either True or False by putting a tick in the relevant column of the table below.

(2 marks)

Statement	True	False
Variable costs change directly with changes in activity		
If a cost is £15 per unit at output of 3,000 units and £5 per unit when output is 9,000 units, the cost is a fixed cost		

(b) Classify the following costs as either fixed or variable by putting a tick in the relevant column of the table below.

(4 marks)

Costs	Fixed	Variable
Chemicals used in making paint		
Wages of machine operators paid at a piecework rate		
Salaries of maintenance workers		
Business rates on a car showroom		

(c)   Jumper Co is trying to decide whether to use an overhead absorption rate based on labour hours or machine hours.

Total factory activity is forecast as follows:

Machine hours   250,000
Labour hours   100,000
Overheads   £600,000

Complete the table below to show the overhead absorption rates based on machine hours and based on labour hours. The absorption rates should be calculated to two decimal places.

(2 marks)

	£
Overhead absorption rate per hour based on machine hours	
Overhead absorption rate per hour based on labour hours	

Task 5 (12 marks)

Watson Ltd makes a single product and has the following production and cost data:

Variable costs   £10 per unit
Fixed costs   £20,000 per month

Watson Ltd can choose to produce 500, 2,500, 5,000 or 7,500 units over its next budget period. It wishes to identify its unit cost at each level of production.

The table below has been partly completed in order to provide expenditure information for the three months.

Complete table by selecting column headings from the picklists. Complete the rows for each production level by inserting figures into the table, correct to two decimal places.

Units produced	Fixed costs	Variable costs £	Total costs	Unit cost £
500	20,000	5,000	25,000	50.00
2,500				
5,000				
7,500				

Task 6 (12 marks)

You are told the opening inventory of a single good for resale in the warehouse is 2,000 units at £20.00 per unit. During the month 3,000 units at £22.00 per unit are received and the following week 3,200 units are issued for sale.

(a) **Identify the valuation method described in the statements below.**   **(3 marks)**

Statement	FIFO	LIFO	AVCO
The closing inventory is valued at £36,000			
The issue of 3,200 units is costed at £67,840			
The closing inventory is valued at £39,600			

You are told the opening inventory of a single good for resale in the warehouse is 2,000 units at £20.00 per unit. During the month 3,000 units at £22.00 per unit are received and the following week 3,200 units are issued for sale.

(b) **Identify whether the statements in the table below are true or false by putting a tick in the relevant column.** **(3 marks)**

Statement	True	False
AVCO values the closing inventory at £38,120		
FIFO costs the issue of 3,200 units at £66,400		
LIFO costs the issue of 3,200 units at £70,000		

Jersey Ltd has the following movements in a certain type of inventory into and out of its stores for the month of July:

Date	Receipts Units	Cost £	Issues Units	Cost £
July 5	1,000	1,500		
July 8	1,500	3,000		
July 12	2,500	6,250		
July 20			3,000	
July 25	2,000	6,000		

(c) **Complete the table below for the issue and closing inventory values.** **(6 marks)**

Method	Cost of issue on 20 July £	Closing inventory at 31 July £
FIFO		
LIFO		
AVCO		

Task 7 (8 marks)

(a) **Identify each labour payment method by putting a tick in the relevant column of the table below.** **(2 marks)**

Payment method	Time-rate	Piecework	Piecework plus bonus
This method acts as an incentive to produce more			
If output is better than expected a bonus is paid			

(b) Exeter Ltd pays a time-rate of £12.50 per hour to its direct labour for a standard 35-hour week. Any of the labour force working in excess of 35 hours is paid an overtime rate of £15 per hour.

Calculate the gross wage for the week for the two workers in the table below. **(6 marks)**

Note. **If no overtime is paid you should enter 0 as the overtime for that worker.**

Worker	Hours worked	Basic wage £	Overtime £	Gross wage £
J Collins	35 hours			
M Thatcher	40 hours			

Task 8 (12 marks)

Churchill Ltd wishes to produce a table detailing budgeted and actual results for last month and showing variances. It had the following budget:

Income   £130,000

Expenditure:

Materials   £33,750
Labour   £35,000
Overheads £30,000

Enter the above data into the table below, calculate the amount of each variance and then determine whether it is adverse or favourable by typing F for favourable and A for adverse in the right-hand column of the table below.

Income/Expenditure	Budget £	Actual £	Variance £	Adverse (A)/Favourable (F)
Income		121,580		
Materials		34,250		
Labour		32,125		
Production overheads		29,812		

Task 9 (12 marks)

Colyton Ltd has the following actual results for the month of February which are to be compared to the budget:

Income   £139,125

Expenditure:
Materials   £20,200
Labour   £56,125
Production overheads   £32,120

Enter the above data into the table below, calculate the amount of each variance and then determine whether it is adverse or favourable by typing F for favourable and A for adverse in the right-hand column of the table below.

Income/Expenditure	Budget £	Actual £	Variance £	Adverse (A) or Favourable (F)
Income	136,500			
Materials	25,500			
Labour	55,000			
Production overheads	35,000			

Task 10 (10 marks)

The following performance table for this month has been produced for Weston. Any variance in excess of 5% of budget is deemed to be significant and should be reported to the relevant manager for review and appropriate action.

Calculate each variance as a percentage of the budgeted amount, correct to one decimal place. Indicate whether each variance is significant or not significant by inserting S or NS.

Expenditure	Budget £	Variance £	Adverse/ Favourable	Variance as percentage of budget %	Significant (S)/ Not significant (NS)
Materials	170,000	8,750	Adverse		
Labour	140,000	9,025	Adverse		
Production overheads	52,000	4,218	Favourable		
Administration overheads	45,000	5,810	Adverse		
Selling and Distribution overheads	22,000	500	Adverse		

BPP PRACTICE ASSESSMENT 3
ELEMENTS OF COSTING

ANSWERS

BPP
LEARNING MEDIA

Elements of Costing
BPP practice assessment 3

Task 1

(a)

Statement	True	False
If prices of materials are rising FIFO will give a higher inventory valuation than LIFO	✓	
A variance is the difference between budgeted and expected cost		✓
In a LIFO system the most recent purchases are assumed to have been issued first	✓	
Financial accounting results in the presentation of financial information for external users	✓	

(b)

Transaction	Capital	Revenue
Purchase of office furniture for office manager	✓	
Purchase of office furniture by office furniture saleroom for resale		✓
Paying VAT		✓
Making cash sales		✓

Task 2

(a)

Cost	Production	Administration	Selling and distribution	Finance
Advertising dinghies in local newspaper			✓	
Material for making sails in the factory	✓			
Fees to estate agent for locating new premises		✓		
Interest charged on long-term loan				✓

(b)

Cost	Fixed	Variable	Semi-variable
Charge for electricity for the kilns firing the pots that includes a standing charge			✓
Annual entertainment budget for the pottery	✓		
Cost of glazes bought in to glaze the pots		✓	
Labour costs for potters paid on a piecework basis		✓	

Task 3

Cost	Code
Wages of delivery driver	3IND
Fees for annual audit by local accountants	3IND
Yeast used in baking at Bakery 1	1DIR
Bakers' salaries at Bakery 2	2DIR
Power used at Bakery 1	1IND

Task 4

(a)

Statement	True	False
Variable costs change directly with changes in activity	✓	
If a cost is £15 per unit at output of 3,000 units and £5 per unit when output is 9,000 units, the cost is a fixed cost	✓	

(b)

Costs	Fixed	Variable
Chemicals used in making paint		✓
Wages of machine operators paid at a piecework rate		✓
Salaries of maintenance workers	✓	
Business rates on a car showroom	✓	

(c)

	£
Overhead absorption rate per hour based on machine hours	2.40
Overhead absorption rate per hour based on labour hours	6.00

Task 5

Units produced	Fixed costs £	Variable costs £	Total costs £	Unit cost £
500	20,000	5,000	25,000	50.00
2,500	20,000	25,000	45,000	18.00
5,000	20,000	50,000	70,000	14.00
7,500	20,000	75,000	95,000	12.67

Task 6

(a)

Statement	FIFO	LIFO	AVCO
The closing inventory is valued at £36,000		✓	
The issue of 3,200 units is costed at £67,840			✓
The closing inventory is valued at £39,600	✓		

(b)

Statement	True	False
AVCO values the closing inventory at £38,120		✓
FIFO costs the issue of 3,200 units at £66,400	✓	
LIFO costs the issue of 3,200 units at £70,000	✓	

Workings

	Units	Per unit £	Total £	Balance £
Opening inventory	2,000	20	40,000	40,000
Received	3,000	22	66,000	106,000
	5,000			
Issued	(3,200)			
Closing inventory	1,800			

	FIFO	LIFO	AVCO
Issue	(2,000 × £20) + (1,200 × £22) = £66,400	(3,000 × £22) + (200 × £20) = £70,000	3,200 × £106,000/5,000 = £67,840
Closing inventory	1,800 × £22 = £39,600	(1,800 × £20) = £36,000	1,800 × £106,000/5,000 = £38,160

(c)

Method	Cost of issue on 20 July £	Closing inventory at 31 July £
FIFO	£1,500 + £3,000 +(500/2,500 × £6,250) = **£5,750**	£6,000 + (2,000/2,500 × £6,250) = **£11,000**
LIFO	£6,250 + (500/1,500 × £3,000) = **£7,250**	£6,000 + £1,500 + (1,000/1,500 × £3,000) = **£9,500**
AVCO	[(£1,500 + £3,000 + £6,250)/5,000] × 3,000 = **£6,450**	£6,000 + [(£1,500 + £3,000 + £6,250)/5,000 × 2,000] = **£10,300**

Task 7

(a)

Payment method	Time-rate	Piecework	Piecework plus bonus
This method acts as an incentive to produce more		✓	
If output is better than expected a bonus is paid			✓

(b)

Worker	Hours worked	Basic wage £	Overtime £	Gross wage £
J Collins	35 hours	437.50	0	437.50
M Thatcher	40 hours	437.50	75.00	512.50

Task 8

Income/ Expenditure	Budget £	Actual £	Variance £	Adverse (A)/ Favourable (F)
Income	130,000	121,580	8,420	A
Materials	33,750	34,250	500	A
Labour	35,000	32,125	2,875	F
Production overheads	30,000	29,812	188	F

Task 9

Income/ Expenditure	Budget £	Actual £	Variance £	Adverse (A) or Favourable (F)
Income	136,500	139,125	2,625	F
Materials	25,500	20,200	5,300	F
Labour	55,000	56,125	1,125	A
Production overheads	35,000	32,120	2,880	F

Task 10

Expenditure	Budget £	Variance £	Adverse/ Favourable	Variance as percentage of budget %	Significant (S)/ Not significant (NS)
Materials	170,000	8,750	Adverse	5.1	S
Labour	140,000	9,025	Adverse	6.4	S
Production overheads	52,000	4,218	Favourable	8.1	S
Administration overheads	45,000	5,810	Adverse	12.9	S
Selling and Distribution overheads	22,000	500	Adverse	2.3	NS

Notes